The Football Book

EXPANDED EDITION

1981 | MEAN JOE GREENE'S STEELERS HELMET

SAMMY BAUGH
Washington Redskins | QB
1938
Photograph by CARL M. MYDANS

BRETT FAVRE
Green Bay Packers | QB
2002
Photograph by WALTER IOOSS JR.

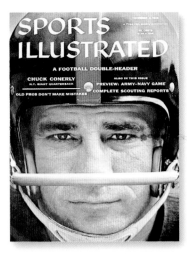

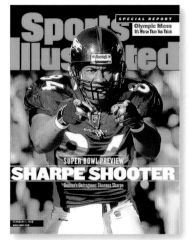

The Football Book
EXPANDED EDITION

ROB FLEDER
Editor

STEVEN HOFFMAN
Designer

DICK FRIEDMAN, BOB ROE, MARK GODICH *Senior Editors*

CRISTINA SCALET, HEATHER BROWN *Photo Editors*

DAVID SABINO *Associate Editor*   ADAM DUERSON, ANDREA WOO *Reporters*

KEVIN KERR *Copy Editor*   JOSH DENKIN *Associate Designer*

THE PRO FOOTBALL HALL OF FAME
Archives and Historical Reference

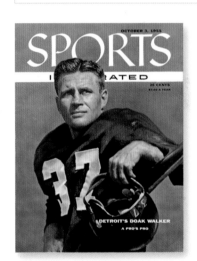

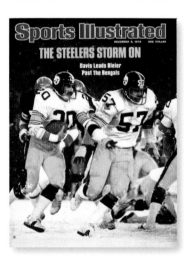

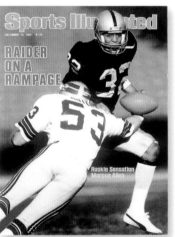

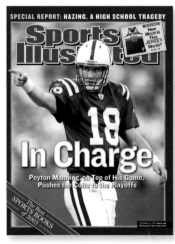

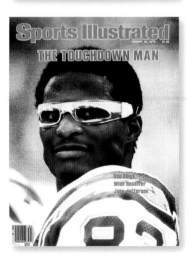

Sports Illustrated

Contents

Y.A. TITTLE'S SHOULDER PADS
(worn throughout his NFL career)
1950–1964
Photograph by DAVID N. BERKWITZ

NFL STARTING QUARTERBACKS
1961
Photograph by RALPH MORSE

(clockwise from top left)

MILT PLUM • 16
Cleveland Browns

BOBBY LAYNE • 22
Pittsburgh Steelers

SAM ETCHEVERRY • 14
St. Louis Cardinals

BILL WADE • 9
Chicago Bears

DON MEREDITH • 17
Dallas Cowboys

FRAN TARKENTON • 10
Minnesota Vikings

JIM NINOWSKI • 15
Detroit Lions

THE KICKOFF
The Colts' Steve Myhra put the boot to The Duke
againts the Bears in Baltimore's Memorial Stadium
1960
Photograph by GEORGE SILK

BOBBY LAYNE, Pittsburgh Steelers, 1958–62

INTRODUCTION

BY AUSTIN MURPHY

FEEL FREE TO MOCK ME

WHILE I DROP A REFERENCE TO PROUST IN A FOOTBALL BOOK. ❧ IT WAS A RIDICULOUS COOKIE, A MADELEINE, THAT TRANSPORTED THE MAIN CHARACTER OF *SWANN'S WAY* BACK TO HIS YOUTH. FOR ME, IT WAS THIS FULL-PAGE PICTURE OF A DISTRESSED STEELERS HELMET.

BILLY SHAW, Buffalo Bills, 1961–69

That half-century-old headgear, it turns out, belonged to Bobby Layne, the notorious night owl who famously alibied, after a wee-hours fender bender, that he'd been minding his own business when his vehicle was struck by "a parked, swerving streetcar."

Layne finished his Hall of Fame career in Pittsburgh, where I grew up, and where my father was an assistant manager of sales for U.S. Steel. So intertwined were the "Stillers" and their fans that it made perfect sense, in 1962, for Art Rooney's outfit to adopt U.S. Steel's "Steelmark" design as its new logo.

When I see those three diamonds, I am transported to Dec. 23, 1972, at Three Rivers Stadium. On that chill afternoon I sat slack-jawed, along with my father, my brother Chris and my uncle Jack, as the rookie Franco Harris tiptoed down the left sideline—he was running toward us—with a ball he'd plucked off his shoestrings on fourth-and-hopeless in a divisional playoff against the Oakland Raiders. I was there for the Immaculate Reception. A watershed moment for one of the proudest franchises in sport served also as a powerful lesson to an 11-year-old boy: Even in the darkest moments, there is always hope.

Thumbing through this trove, this reliquary, this box of madeleines, I stopped at page 314, mesmerized by the head-slap meted out by the late, great Minister of Defense, Reggie White, to a Tennessee Oiler named Frank Wycheck. The victim's neck is twisted unnaturally; you can almost hear the ringing in his ears.

That photo made me recall ex-Steelers guard Craig (Wolf Man) Wolfley remembering his first meeting with White. It was 1988, White's fourth season with the Philadelphia Eagles. The Steelers ran a trap at White on their first play. "I pull," said Wolfley, the left guard, "and Reggie's coming off [right tackle] Tunch Ilkin's butt. Reggie drops to a knee. He's gonna squeeze the trap." A salty vet who'd seen this "groundhog" maneuver before, Wolfley was ready with a countermeasure. "I thought I'd cross-face him"—rake a forearm across the reverend's face—"and dig him out with a knee to the ribs," Wolfley recalled. "But he somehow got underneath me, stood up, and just launched me about 10 feet. On the bright side, he threw me in the direction of the huddle, so I didn't have far to walk."

Wolfley shared this reminiscence at the 2007 NFL combine in the Indianapolis Convention Center. He is now a radio broadcaster in Pittsburgh. We were chatting outside the

NFL Network's Total Access room, where pro prospects go on camera and answer such hard-hitting questions as "Who are you off the field?" and "Where do you find your strength?" Then, with cameras rolling, they are invited to dance.

This is after they've been drug-tested and interrogated by NFL security types, then stripped to their skivvies and paraded on a stage in front of an auditorium full of scouts, then taken a seat in the Bod Pod, which measures their percentage of body fat.

"Can you imagine Artie Donovan in the Bod Pod?" I asked Wolfley, and we had a good laugh. Then he cut straight to the heart of the issue. "When you take all this away," said the Wolf Man, his sweeping gesture encompassing the hovering agents, the would-be financial advisers and the Total Access room, "the game hasn't changed so much. At the end of the day, football's football."

They can turn the combine into a surreal pageant, in other words; can slap visors on helmets and microphones on zebras, and suspend Skycams above the huddle. But they cannot alter the essence of this game. That is the theme running through this book like a Gale Sayers kickoff return. Yes, you will find many delightful, provocative illustrations of pro football's evolution (check out Joe Namath's primitive knee brace on page 86). At the same time, like a Chuck Noll counter-trap, the voices accompanying those images—the prose of some of the finest football writers ever—admonish us not to always believe our eyes.

While the salaries have grown and the cheerleaders' uniforms have shrunk, the overriding objective remains very much the same as it was in the 1920s, when Indian Joe Guyon turned on a Chicago Bear named George Halas, who was coming for him on a crackback block. "When he got close, I wheeled around and nailed him, goddam," Guyon tells the late Myron Cope on page 32. "Broke three of his ribs. And as they carried him off I said to him, 'What the hell, Halas? Don't you know you can't sneak up on an Indian?'"

Which is the more politically incorrect: Guyon trafficking in stereotypes about native Americans, or the guilty pleasure we take in accounts and images of such mayhem?

Our hearts soar, of course, at the montage of grace notes depicted in these pages: the artistry of Randy Moss and Jerry Rice; the balletic contortions of Lynn Swann, the fingertip

> THE IMMACULATE RECEPTION SERVED AS A POWERFUL LESSON TO AN 11-YEAR-OLD BOY: EVEN IN THE DARKEST MOMENTS, THERE IS ALWAYS HOPE.

ART SHELL, Oakland & L.A. Raiders, 1968–82

Catch by Dwight Clark that midwifed a dynasty. But even to this ex-Colgate jayvee wide receiver, the irresistible appeal of this tome, aside from its sublime writing, is that it serves as a compilation of football's greatest hits.

Literally. There, for instance, is Frank Gifford's cartoon-violent, November 1960 rendezvous with one Chuck Bednarik, in which Concrete Charlie knocks the gentlemanly New York Giant into 1962. By which we mean, Gifford missed the rest of the '60 campaign, and all of '61, before courageously returning to the NFL for three more seasons.

"It was like when you hit a home run," says Bednarik, recalling that collision for John Schulian on page 48, "and you say, 'Geez, I didn't even feel it hit the bat.'"

There is an element of rubbernecking in our compulsion to review—indeed, to revel in—such havoc. To the men in the arena the appeal runs deeper. Football is, in plain terms, a license to commit battery, "controlled violence," as Conrad Dobler puts it to Daphne Hurford on page 148, "mixed with careful technical planning."

Even that description sanitized the vocation of Dobler, a.k.a. Vlad the Impaler, long recognized as the dirtiest player in NFL history. Asked if there was any truth to reports that he made a habit of biting opponents, Dobler answers Hurford's question with a rhetorical question of his own. "If someone stuck...his fingers in your mouth, what would you do?"

After Texas Tech knocked off No. 1 Texas on Nov. 1, 2008, I drew Tech coach Mike Leach out on the subject of Colby Whitlock, a nosetackle whose cleat marks could be found, following the game, on the flak vest of Longhorns quarterback Colt McCoy.

"He likes combat," replied Leach, cutting to the core of the matter, "and is lucky enough to be able to engage in it legally."

Now we are hewing close to the true appeal of this game, which, at its most elemental, is a glorified brawl, "a Neanderthal struggle," in the words of Paper Lion George Plimpton, who must be the only quarterback in history to remind himself, as he does on page 134, "You must not dally, son. On the handoffs you must get the ball to the halfbacks with dispatch."

Around the time I was happily immersing myself in these pages, I was rereading Cormac McCarthy's *Blood Meridian*, whose cover blurb proclaims it "a classic American novel of

regeneration through violence," a passage that left me asking myself, What the hell is that supposed to mean? Shedding light on the matter is Rick Telander, whose essay *The Last Angry Men* (page 72) is a penetrating meditation on linebackers and the ill will they share, like mitochondrial DNA. In it Telander asks Dick Butkus, Why so angry?

It's not really anger, Butkus explains. It's more a desire to set things right, to prove to ballcarriers and quarterbacks that "you don't get something for nothing." In football, in other words, the brutality is a means to some end, the settling of scores, the meting out of Old Testament justice. Violence "can resolve ambivalence and uncertainty," Telander concludes. "And who doesn't crave certainty in life, a reward for the good, punishment for the bad?"

Who doesn't crave clarity, catharsis, *regeneration*? The most indelible passage from *Blood Meridian*, for my money, is that of an ambush of a band of U.S. scalp hunters by a Comanche war party, "a legion of horribles...all the horseman's faces grotesque with daubings like a company of mounted clowns, death hilarious...riding down upon them like a horde from a hell more horrible yet than the brimstone land of Christian reckoning."

That postcard of a nightmare prefigured Paul Zimmerman's lead from Super Bowl XX (page 166), which begins: "It will be many years before we see anything approaching the vision of hell that Chicago inflicted on the poor New England Patriots...." True, Dr. Z's strong opinions and general obstreperousness might result in a few tense moments around a dinner table with some of his fellow writers. (Take my word for it.) But it is that same cocksure contrarian's conviction, grounded in a rarely surpassed knowledge of the game, that makes him one of the best football scribes, ever.

Yes, the Bears routed New England that day, 46–10. But rather than carping about anticlimax, a route taken by many of his peers, Zim zeroed in on the historic nature of Chicago's defensive dominance: "The game wasn't exciting. So what?... Nor was the British cavalry charge at Balaklava, but Tennyson wrote a poem about it. This game transcended the ordinary standards we use in judging football."

So do the writing and photography featured in the pages that follow transcend their genre. Prepare to be transported.

> FOOTBALL IS A LICENSE TO COMMIT BATTERY, "CONTROLLED VIOLENCE," AS DOBLER SAID, "MIXED WITH CAREFUL TECHNICAL PLANNING."

The Ga

2005 | ALWAYS LIKELY to catch any ball within reach, the Bengals' Chad Johnson
was bumped off this one by the Browns' Brian Russell | *Photograph by* THOMAS E. WITTE

1976 | STEELERS WIDEOUT Lynn Swann laid out the Cowboys in Super Bowl X in Miami, and was the game's MVP | *Photograph by* HEINZ KLUETMEIER

1982 | DWIGHT CLARK'S last-minute catch beat the Cowboys and put the 49ers in the Super Bowl | *Photograph by* WALTER IOOSS JR.

1960 | JIM TAYLOR could grind out yardage for Green Bay even when the tundra wasn't frozen | *Photograph by* HY PESKIN

c. 1960 | PACKERS TACKLE Forrest Gregg, whom Vince Lombardi called "the best player I ever coached" | *Photograph by* VERNON BIEVER

1973 | O.J. SIMPSON broke Jim Brown's single-season rushing record with this carry, and ended the season with 2,003 yards | *Photograph by* NEIL LEIFER

1972 | LARRY CSONKA (39) was the battering ram for a Miami team that won back-to-back Super Bowls | *Photograph by* NEIL LEIFER

1970 | TOM DEMPSEY, though born with half his right foot missing, set an NFL record with this 63-yard field goal; his kicking shoe is in the Hall of Fame | *Photograph by* AP *(right)*

2008 | TIGHT END Delanie Walker (46) of the 49ers hit paydirt, but he and Bryant Johnson would see a penalty wipe away the touchdown | *Photograph by* JED JACOBSOHN

THE GAME THAT WAS

BY MYRON COPE

Some of the NFL's pioneers recall, in their own words, the league's wild and uncertain early days, when one team promoted its New York games by having players ride horses down Broadway and a $1 investment could yield $1.5 million. —*from* SI, OCTOBER 13 & 20, 1969

INDIAN JOE GUYON
(1919–1927: Canton Bulldogs, Cleveland Indians, Oorang Indians, Rock Island Independents, Kansas City Cowboys, New York Giants)
The late Ralph McGill, the distinguished Atlanta newspaper publisher and author, once wrote, "There is no argument about the identity of the greatest football player who ever performed in Dixie. There is a grand argument about second place, but for first place there is Joe Guyon, the Chippewa brave."

I PLAYED halfback on offense, and on defense I played sideback, which I suppose is what they later started calling defensive halfback. I had more damn tricks and, brother, I could hit you. Elbows, knees or whatchamacallit—boy, I could use 'em. Yes, and it's true that I used to laugh like the dickens when I saw other players get injured. Self-protection is the first thing they should have learned. You take care of yourself, you know. I think it's a sin if you don't. It's a rough game, so you've got to *equip* yourself and know what to do.

The games that were real scraps were the ones in Chicago. George Halas was a brawler. There'd be a fight every time we met those sons of biscuits. Halas knew that I was the key man. He knew that getting me out of there would make a difference. I was playing defense one time, and I saw him coming after me from a long ways off. I was always alert. But I pretended I didn't see him. When he got close I wheeled around the nailed him, goddam. Broke three of his ribs. And as they carried him off I said to him, "What the hell, Halas. Don't you know you can't sneak up on an Indian?"

ED HEALEY
(1920–1927: Rock Island Independents, Chicago Bears)
IN 1922 the Rock Island Independents sold me to the Chicago Bears following a game that I remember as clearly as if it were just played today. We had a great team! We had lost just once. And on the Sunday prior to Thanksgiving we played the Bears at Wrigley Field.

Now understand, in Chicago the officialdom was such that on occasion it made it a little difficult for the outsider to win. On this day the game was really a tight one. In fact, it was going along 0–0. George Halas, who along with Dutch Sternaman owned the Bears and played for them, was at right end, the opponent for myself, who was the left tackle. Halas had a habit of grabbing ahold of my jersey, see? My sleeve. That would throw me a little off my balance. It would twist me just enough so that my head wasn't going where I was going.

I didn't enjoy being the victim with reference to this holding, so I forewarned him of what I intended to do about it. Likewise it was necessary for me to forewarn the head linesman, whose name was Roy. I said, "Now, Roy, I understand to start with that you're on the payroll of the Bears. I know that your eyesight must be failing you, because this man Halas is holding me on occasion and it is completely destroying all the things that I'm designed to do." I said, "Roy, in the event that Halas holds me again I am going to commit mayhem."

Now bear in mind, please, that we had a squad of about 15 or 16 men. Neither Duke Slater, our right tackle, nor I had a substitute on the bench. So I said, "Roy, you can't put me out of the game, because we don't have another tackle. And I can't really afford to be put out of this ball game because of your failure to call Halas's holding. I have notified him, and now I am about to commit mayhem."

Well, the condition of the field was muddy and slippery—a very unsafe field. Halas pulled his little trick once more, and I come across with a right, because his head was going to my right. Fortunately for him he slipped, and my fist went whizzing straight into the terra firma, which was soft and mucky. My fist was buried. When I pulled it out it was with an effort like a suction pump.

This was on a Sunday, and on the following Tuesday, I believe it was, I was told to report to the Bears. George Halas had bought me for $100.

Three years later, on a Saturday prior to Thanksgiving 1925 Red Grange performed in his last game for Illinois. He played against Ohio State at Columbus, then took the sleeper to Chicago and the next day he joined the Bears. And then, with Grange as the main attraction, we set out on a trip and exploded the Eastern Coast, playing by day and hopping to the next city by overnight sleeper. Of course, we did not always play up to our capability, because the human body can stand just so much. But the Redhead broke away in Philadel-

RED GRANGE brought the credibility of the college game to the pros when he signed with the Bears in 1925.

phia on a Saturday. He broke away in New York on Sunday.

With Red Grange, a gentleman and a scholar, we exploded not only the Eastern Coast but likewise the Western Coast and the South with the introduction of professional football. . . .

RED GRANGE
(1925–1934: Chicago Bears, New York Yankees)

Alone among all the players of the pro football decades that preceded television, Grange earned from football the six-figure income that stars of the 1960s were to realize. Behind his early financial success was that unique operator, C.C. (Cash & Carry) Pyle, probably the first players' agent known to football. It was the Roaring Twenties, the Golden Age of Sport, and with Pyle calling the shots Grange became the plutocrat of football. He fondly remembers Cash & Carry.

CHARLIE PYLE was about 44 years old when I met him. He was the most dapper man I have ever seen. He went to the barbershop every day of his life. He had a little mustache that he'd have trimmed, and he would have a manicure and he'd have his hair trimmed up a little, and every day he would get a rubdown. He wore a derby and spats and carried a cane, and believe me, he was a handsome guy. The greatest ladies' man that ever lived.

Money was of no consequence to Charlie.

At this particular time he owned three movie theaters—two in Champaign, Ill. and one in Kokomo, Ind. One night during my senior year at Illinois I went down to the Virginia Theater in Champaign and one of the ushers told me, "Mr. Pyle wants to see you in his office." Well, the first words Charlie Pyle said to me were, "Red, how would you like to make $100,000?" I couldn't figure what he was talking about. But he said, "I have a plan. I will go out and set up about 10 or 12 football games throughout the United States."

Of course I was flabbergasted. But Charlie made good his word. He lined it up for me to play with the Bears and then went out on the road and set up the whole program.

I'll never forget the game we played in Coral Gables outside of Miami, at a time when Florida was swinging. In 1925 everybody there was selling real estate and building things. Three days before the game we looked around, and there was no place to play a football game, so we said, "Where are we going to play?" The people told us, "Out here in this field." Well, there wasn't anything there except a field. But two days before the game they put 200 carpenters to work and built a wooden stadium that seated 25,000. They sold tickets ranging up to $20 apiece, and the next day they tore down the stadium. You'd never know a ball game had taken place there.

One thing about Charlie was that he always thought pro football had a future. I didn't. When I played, outside of the franchise towns nobody knew anything about pro ball. A U.S. Senator took me to the White House once and introduced me to Calvin Coolidge and said, "Mr. President, I want you to meet Red Grange. He's with the Chicago Bears." I remember the President's reply very well. He said, "Well, Mr. Grange, I'm glad to meet you. I have always liked animal acts."

OLE HAUGSRUD
(1926–1927: Owner, Duluth Eskimos)

Originally the Duluth club was a fine semipro outfit called the Kelley-Duluths, having been named for the Kelley-Duluth Hardware Store. The Kelley-Duluths' opposition came largely from teams in nearby towns in the iron-ore range. But in 1923, in order to obtain a professional schedule, Dan Williams and three others—the trainer and two players—put up $250 apiece and bought a National Football League franchise for $1,000. Even then, the renamed Duluth Eskimos were able to arrange no more than seven, and sometimes as few as five, league games a season. Bills piled up. Finally the four owners offered to make a gift of the franchise to Ole Haugsrud, the club's secretary-treasurer. To make the transaction legal, Haugsrud handed them a dollar, which the four men immediately squandered drinking nickel beer. The dollar they paid for those 20 beers would be one Dan Williams and his colleagues would never forget.

The year was 1926, and the struggling NFL was fighting for its life. C.C. Pyle had Red Grange under contract and with Grange as his box-office attraction was formulating his new nine-team league, to be known as the American Football League. Pyle spread the word that he also had signed the celebrated All-America back, Ernie Nevers, a handsome blond who, though just emerging from Stanford, had captured the nation's fancy. The NFL knew Nevers to be the only big name with whom the league could salvage its slim prestige, but NFL club owners took Pyle at his word, and they made no effort to sign Nevers.

Alone, Ole Haugsrud, a mild-looking little Swede, was skeptical. He had been a high-school classmate of Ernie Nevers in Superior, Wis. When he paid a dollar for the Duluth franchise he had it in the back of his mind to travel to St. Louis, where Nevers was pitching for the St. Louis Browns, to see for himself if Pyle actually had Nevers under contract.

ERNIE WAS very glad to see me, and I was glad to see him. I met with him and his wife at their apartment, and Ernie showed me a letter he had from C.C. Pyle. Ernie told me,

JOE GUYON, who starred on both sides of the ball for the Canton Bulldogs, liked to play rough and didn't apologize for that.

"Ole, if you can meet the terms Pyle is offering in this letter, it's O.K. with me. I'll play for Duluth." And, really, that's all there was to it. I would have to pay Ernie $15,000 plus a percentage of the larger gates. I didn't pay him five cents to sign. Oh, maybe I gave him a dollar to make it legal, but really a handshake was all Ernie wanted. A handshake with an old friend was good enough for Ernie.

The league meeting was at the Morrison Hotel, and it was getting on close to August, I believe. See, they didn't hold meetings way ahead of the season, because a lot of teams didn't know if they could operate for another year, and they had to get some funds behind them before they could go to a meeting.

In Chicago the first fellows I got hold of were Tim Mara of the New York Giants and George Halas of the Bears. I had called Tim Mara prior to that, and he was really the only one who knew about the contract I had with Ernie Nevers.

This was kind of a historic point for the National League, because here everybody was, with the threat that Pyle had hanging over them, and the league really didn't know if it was going to operate again. So Mara said to me, "Wait till I highball you, and then you go up to the league president with your option on Nevers." Well, I waited and watched Mara, and when he signaled I took the option up to Joe Carr, who was being paid $500 to be league president. He read that little document and then looked up and said: "Gentlemen, I got a surprise for you!" He read the option paper aloud, and some of them out front got up and yelled like a bunch of kids. Carr said to me, "You've saved the league!"

There was almost a celebration right there. But Tim Mara said, "Gentlemen, we got to make a league out of this, so we'll start all over by first rehiring the president and paying him a salary that means something."

Then Mara said, "Now let's start over and get a new schedule. "Well, we started putting down that 1926 schedule, and now everybody wanted to play me. I had 19 league games as fast as I could write them down. Before I got back to Duluth I had 10 exhibition games, too, which made a total of 29. And all because I had Nevers.

Mr. Mara got up and said, "What we've got to do is to fill the ball parks in the big cities. So we've got to make road teams out of the Duluth Eskimos and the Kansas City Cowboys." He knew we would draw the big-city crowds with Ernie, and the Kansas City Cowboys were good at drawing crowds because they had a gimmick. When they arrived in a town they'd borrow a lot of horses and ride them down the main street. They rode horseback down Broadway and drew 39,000 people in New York.

So we had only two home games—one in Duluth and one over in Superior, where the ball park had railroad tracks on both sides. The railroad men would leave boxcars lined up there. We drew 3,000 or 4,000 at the box office in Superior, but there were just as many standing on the boxcars watching free.

I believe it was September 6th that we hit the road, and we didn't get back until February 5th. We traveled by train and occasionally by bus, and one time we took a boat from New York to Providence. During one stretch we played five games in eight days, with a squad of 17 men.

After that '27 season, I put the club in mothballs, and then I sold the franchise for $2,000. . . .

But I didn't do so bad by selling. You see, we negotiated the deal at a league meeting in Cleveland, and the fellows from the other clubs were anxious to see it settled and get away, because they didn't always have money enough to stay three, four days in a high-priced hotel. I wanted $3,000 but the fellow wanted to give me $2,000. The others said to me, "Come on, Swede. We got to get going home."

So I said, "All right, but with one stipulation. The next time a franchise is granted in the state of Minnesota I will have the first opportunity to bid for it."

In 1961, when the Minnesota Vikings were created, I got 10% of the stock. The franchise cost $600,000, and I paid $60,000. Since then we've had offers of between $12 million and $15 million for the franchise. So I guess you would have to say that as result of originally buying a franchise for a dollar, and later investing $60,000, I now own stock that is worth about a million and a half.

BULLDOG TURNER
(1940–1952: Chicago Bears)

In 1941, only a year after he had turned pro with the Chicago Bears, he became the first man in nine years to unseat the great Mel Hein of the New York Giants as the NFL's All-League center. Men who played against Turner say that among his virtuosities must be included exquisite stealth in the art of holding.

HERE WAS George Halas's method of operation in practice. First he'd say, "Give me a center!" Then he'd say, "Bausch!" He'd say, "Give me two guards!" Then he'd say, "Fortmann and Musso!" Well, the first time I heard Halas say, "Give me a center!" I didn't wait for nothing more and ran out there and got over the ball. I noticed he looked kind of funny at me, but I didn't think anything about it. I found out later that Pete Bausch was the center—a big, broad, mean ol' ballplayer, a real nice German

PAPA BEAR George Halas was a pioneer in the NFL, first as a scrappy player and then as the often flinty owner of the Chicago Bears.

from Kansas. But all I knew was George had drafted me No. 1 and I had signed a contract to play center, and I thought when it come time to line up I should *be* at center. From the beginning I was overendowed with self-confidence. I feared no man. So I just went out there and got over that ball, and I was there ever since. They didn't need Pete no more.

I was such a good blocker that the men they put in front of me—and some of them were stars that were supposed to be making a lot of tackles—they would have their coaches saying, "Why ain't you making any tackles?" They'd say, "That bum Turner is holding!" Well, that wasn't true. I held a few, but I was blocking them too. I used to think I could handle anybody that they'd put in front of me.

One guy I remember was big Ed Neal. There in the late 1940s he played at Green Bay, and by this time they had put in the 5–4 defense. They put the biggest, toughest guy they had right in front of the center, and I was expected to block him either way. Well, Ed Neal weighed 303 pounds stripped. His arms was as big as my leg and just as hard as that table. He could tell when I was going to center the ball, and he'd get right over it and hit me in the face. You didn't have a face guard then, and so Ed Neal broke my nose seven times. Yes, that's right. No—he broke my nose *five* times. I got it broke seven times, but five times *he* broke it.

Anyway, I got where I'd center that ball and duck my head, so then he started hitting me on top of the headgear. He would beat hell out of my head. We had those headgears that were made out of composition of some kind—some sort of fiber—and I used to take three of them to Green Bay. These headgears would just crack when he'd hit 'em— they'd just ripple across there like lightening had struck them. So there one day, every time Neal went by me I'd grab him by the leg, and I began to get him worried. He said, "You s.o.b., quit holding me!" I said, "If you'll quit hitting me on the head, I'll quit holding you." And Neal said, "That's a deal, 'cause I ain't making no tackles." So the second half of that game we got along good, and later I got Halas to trade for him.

I don't know if you want to put this in your book, and I don't care if you do, but I originated the draw play, along with a lot of other plays. I discovered the draw play because Buckets Goldenberg, who played for Green Bay, could read our quarterback, Sid Luckman, real well. Somehow he could tell when Sid was going to pass. As soon as that ball was snapped, Buckets Goldenberg would pull back and start covering the

pass. So I said, "Let's fake a pass and give the ball to the fullback and let him come right up here where I am, 'cause there's nobody here but me." The next year we put that play in, and it averaged 33 yards a try. The fullback would run plumb to the safety man before they knew he had the ball.

I also originated a play that got me even with Ed Neal for beating my head off. I said to Halas one day, "You can run somebody right through there, 'cause Ed Neal is busy whupping my head." I suggested that we put in a sucker play—we called it the 32 sucker—where we double-teamed both of their tackles and I would just relax and let Neal knock me on my back and fall all over me. It'd make a hole from here to that fireplace. Man, you could really run through it, and we did all day. Later Ralph Jones, who had once been a Bears coach and was coaching a little college team, told me he brought his whole team down to watch the Bears play the Packers that day, and he told them, "Boys, I want you to see the greatest football player that ever lived, Bulldog Turner. I want you to watch this man on every play and see how he handles those guys." But ol' Ralph didn't know about that sucker play, and later he said to me, "Damn if you wasn't flat on your back all day!"

ART ROONEY
(1933– : Owner, Pittsburgh Steelers)
The down-to-earth, ward-loving, last-hurrah millionaire president of the Pittsburgh Steelers, Arthur J. Rooney is one of the supreme contradictions in sport. Perhaps the most successful horseplayer America has ever known—he is said to have won a quarter of a million dollars in a single day—he is professional football's champion loser. In 35 years his team has never earned so much as a divisional title.

Like George Halas, Rooney once played as a pro himself. His team was called Hope-Harvey. He founded it, owned it, coached it and even halfbacked it against the likes of Jim Thorpe and the Canton Bulldogs. Sometimes he was a winner in his Hope-Harvey days, but then. . . .

IN 1933 I paid $2,500 for a National Football League franchise, which I named the Pirates because the Pittsburgh baseball team was called the Pirates. It wasn't until 1940, when we held a contest for a new name, that we became the Steelers. Joe Carr's girlfriend won the contest. There were people who said, "That contest don't look like it was on the level."

I bought the franchise because I figured it would be good to have a league schedule and that eventually professional football would be a big sport. The reason I bought at that particular time was that we knew Pennsylvania was going to repeal some of its blue laws, which had prevented Sunday football.

BULLDOG TURNER, who signed his first pro contract in 1940, played linebacker and was a perennial All-NFL center for the Bears.

The laws were changed, but a couple of days before our opening game the mayor phoned me and said, "I got a complaint here from a preacher that this game should not be allowed. The blue-law repeal hasn't been ratified yet by the city council."

The mayor told me he didn't know what I could do about it, but that I should go see a fellow named Harmar Denny, who was director of public safety and over the police department.

But this Denny was pretty much of a straitlaced guy. All he would say was that he was going away for the weekend. "Good," I told him. "You go away." Then I went to see the superintendent of police, a man named McQuade, and told him my problem.

"Oh, that there's ridiculous," he said. "Give me a couple of tickets and I'll go to the game Sunday. That'll be the last place they'll look for me if they want me to stop the thing." So McQuade hid out at the game, and Pittsburgh got started in the NFL.

The biggest mistake I've made was that, although I understood the football business as well as anybody, I didn't pay the attention to it that some of the other owners did.

I still believe that John Blood could have been a tremendous coach if he would have just paid attention. We once played a game in Los Angeles and John missed the train home. John was known to enjoy a good time, of course, so we didn't see him the whole week. On Sunday he stopped off in Chicago to see his old team, the Green Bay Packers, play the Bears. The newspaper guys asked him, "How come you're not with your team?" And John said, "Oh, we're not playing this week." Well, no sooner did he get those words out of his mouth than the guy on the loudspeaker announced a score. Philadelphia 14, Pittsburgh 7. You really couldn't depend on John a whole lot.

We've had a lot of great ballplayers, you know. Just think of the quarterbacks. We've had Sid Luckman, Earl Morrall, Len Dawson, Jackie Kemp, Bill Nelsen. I'd say we were experts on quarterbacks at Pittsburgh. We had them all, and we got rid of every one of them. We had Johnny Unitas in for a tryout, but our coach then, Walter Kiesling, let him go. Kies said, "He can't remember the plays. He's dumb." You had to know Kies. He was a great coach, but he thought a lot of ballplayers were dumb. We were arguing about a guy one day, and I said, "I don't care how dumb he is. He can run and he can pass and he can block. If he can do those three things, he don't have to be a Rhodes scholar." But all Kies said to that was, "He's dumb."

SAMMY BAUGH
(1937–1952: Washington Redskins)
Starting in 1937, he lasted 16 years and is held by many to have

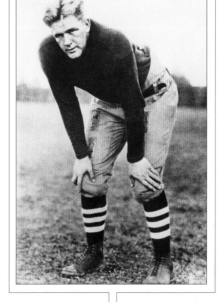

been the finest passer of his or any other time. In one season ('45) he completed 70.3% of his passes. In addition, his leg was as potent as his arm; he holds almost every punting record in the book. But above all, he gave to pro football a radical concept that he had learned from his college coach at Texas Christian, Dutch Meyer—namely, that the forward pass could be more than just a surprise weapon or a desperation tactic. Sammy Baugh made the pass a routine scrimmage play.

THE THING that hurt when I first came into pro football in 1937 was that the rules didn't give any protection to passers. Those linemen could hit the passer until the whistle blew. If you completed a pass out there and somebody's running 50 yards with the ball, well, that bunch could still hit you. In other words, a passer had to learn to throw and *move*. You would never see him just throw and stand there looking. You had to throw and start protecting yourself, because those linemen were going to lay you flatter than the ground every time.

If you were a good ballplayer—a passer or whatever—they tried to hurt you and get you out of there. We had only 22 or 23 men on a squad, and your ballplayers were playing both ways—offense and defense—so if you lost two good ones, you were dead. Well, every now and then they'd run what they called a "bootsie" play, and everybody'd hit one man and just try to tear him to pieces. The object was to get him out of there. I don't mean they ran this kind of play very often, but if they came up against a guy that was giving them a lot of trouble, along would come the bootsie.

I guess it was my third year, 1939, that we finally got the rule protecting the passer. Pro football was changing by then. Back in the '30s it was more of a defensive game. In other words, when you picked your starters, they usually had to be good on defense first. Take the New York Giants. They had such a good defensive ball club that they wouldn't mind punting to you on third down from practically anywhere. They'd kick the ball to you 'cause they didn't think you were ever going to move it.

The fact is, most men played pro football in those days because they liked football. A lot of players today say they only play for the money, but even now, it's not all money. I don't care if salaries went back down, they'd still play. Of course, nobody was making a lot of money out of football in the '30s. That's why I'll always think a lot of George Marshall and George Halas and Art Rooney and those kind of people—they stayed in there when it was rough. They made a great game out of it. . . .

ERNIE NEVERS, the star running back out of Stanford, was the big draw that saved the fledgling NFL after Grange started his own league in 1926.

1994 | THE BEARS' Chris Zorich felt the chill of 15° weather in December, in Green Bay | *Photograph by* JOHN BIEVER

1997 | BRYAN COX didn't lose his head as a linebacker for the Bears. One reason: his massive neck pad | *Photograph by* DAVID LIAM KYLE

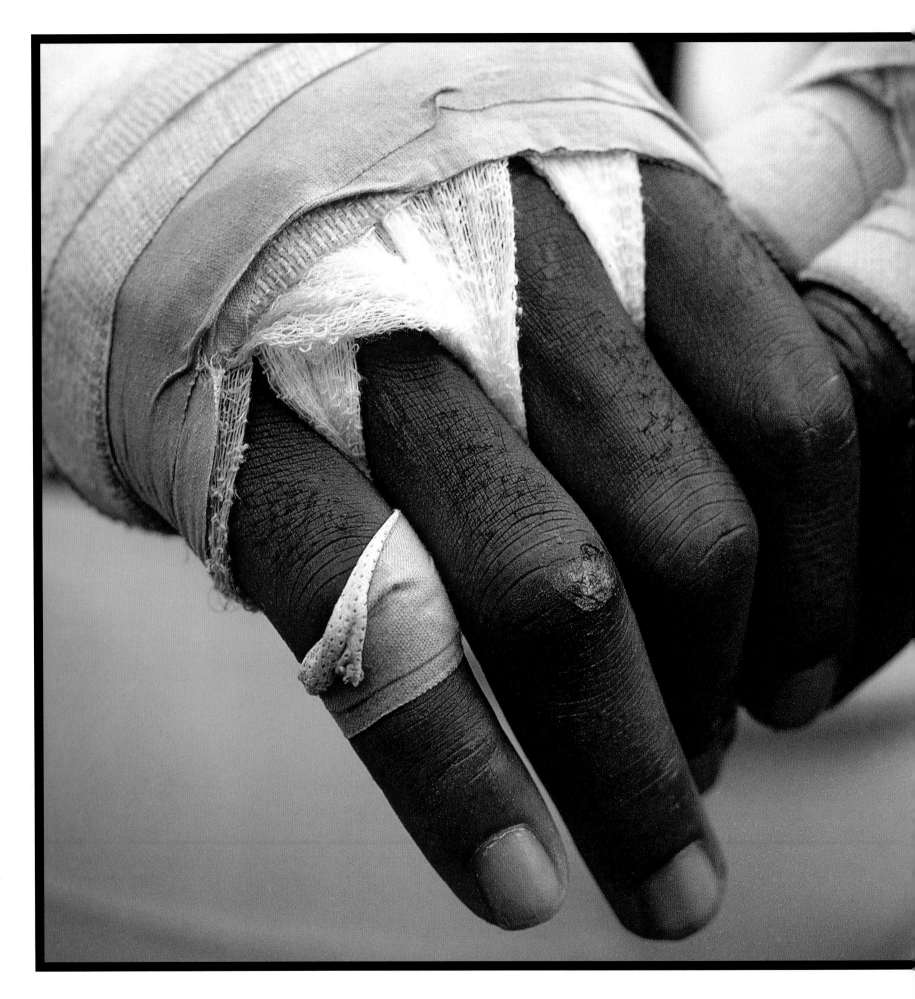

from HOW DOES IT REALLY FEEL? | BY ROY BLOUNT JR.

SI August 12, 1974

O NE AFTERNOON DURING practice I was watching the linemen pound away at each other—*wump, clack.* Guard Bruce Van Dyke paused to say, "What are you doing?" ❧ "Trying to get a feel for this," I said. ❧ "If you really want to get a feel for it you should put on some pads and get out here and get blocked," he said.

"Well," I said, "I thought I would get a feel for it by asking *you* how it feels."

"I try not to notice how it feels," he said. "If you felt it, you wouldn't do it."

I admired coach Chuck Noll's response when a reporter came up to him after the Steelers' loss to Cincinnati and asked, "How do you feel?"

"It hasn't changed," said Noll. "I still feel with my hands."

So I thought I might try treating the question of how football feels by asking players about their hands. One conclusion I was led to from that line of questioning was that football feels terrible. On the backs of their hands and on their knuckles many of the players had wounds of a kind I have never seen on anyone else: fairly deep digs and gouges that were not scabbed over so much as dried. They looked a little like old sores on horses. The body must have given up trying to refill those gouges and just rinded them over and accepted them.

I've never broken a finger," said Mean Joe Greene. "I had 'em stepped on, twisted, but not broken. One time I grabbed at Jim Plunkett and my little finger caught in a twist of his jersey and he ran for a ways dragging me that way, by my little finger. That turned my little finger around, but it didn't break it."

In '72 L.C. Greenwood looked down in the midst of a play to see his middle finger twisted around backward and crossed over the ring finger. "I couldn't figure out what had happened." He had it splinted and played with the splint on, and now that finger sticks out at a grotesque angle. He said he would get it straightened after he was out of football; no point doing it until then.

Most of the defensive linemen had broken *many* fingers. "You can't play football, I don't care what position, without hands," said Dwight White. "I use 'em to pull, knock down, grab. Hands are as important as eyes." He glanced down at his. "See this fanger?" he said. "I got it jammed five years ago, and it's just started to straighten out. See that fanger? Can't wear a ring on it. I got some of the ugliest fangers in the world." . . .

1973 | THE MAYHEM of football took a toll on the hands of L.C. Greenwood.

Photograph by WALTER IOOSS JR.

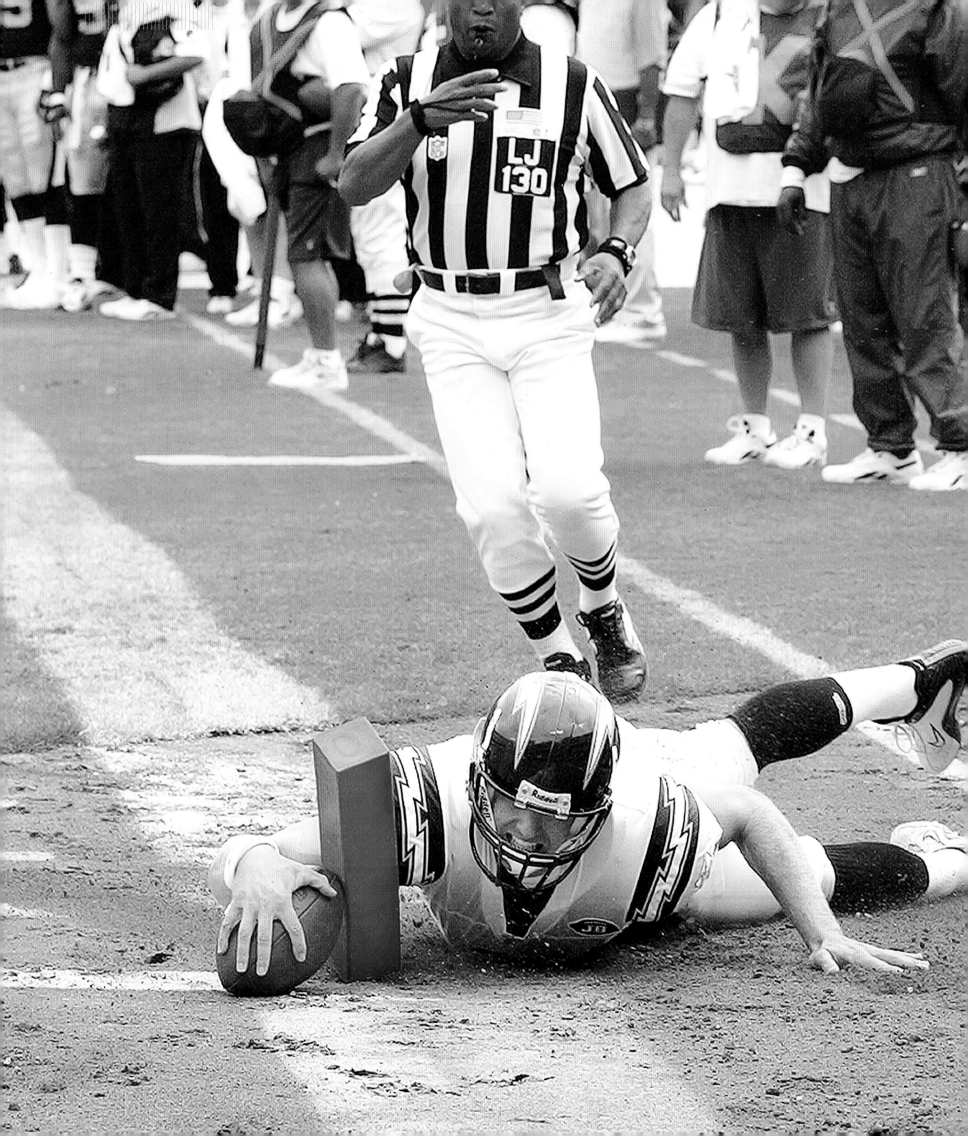

2003 | CHARGERS QUARTERBACK Drew Brees had no margin for error after catching
a 21-yard TD pass from LaDainian Tomlinson | Photograph by JOHN W. MCDONOUGH

> **Artifacts**

Crown Jewels

Before there were Super Bowl rings for every player to covet, there were all manner of other precious mementoes awarded to championship teams as tokens of their victory

1922 | CANTON BULLDOGS CHARM

1941 | CHICAGO BEARS CHARM

1954 | CLEVELAND BROWNS WATCH

1948 | CLEVELAND BROWNS TIE-CLIP

1905 | THE CANTON BULLDOGS, the pro game's first dynasty, won titles in their first two NFL seasons, 1922 and '23

2009 | THREE CARDINALS defenders could only look on helplessly as Super Bowl XLIII MVP
Santonio Holmes made the catch and stayed inbounds for the Steelers' winning score | *Photograph by* JOHN BIEVER

CONCRETE CHARLIE

BY JOHN SCHULIAN

Chuck Bednarik, the last of the 60-minute men, was a stalwart at both linebacker and center but will be known forever for one play, the Tackle. — *from* SI, SEPTEMBER 6, 1993

THE PASS WAS BEHIND Gifford. It was a bad delivery under the best of circumstances, life-threatening where he was now, crossing over the middle. But Gifford was too much the pro not to reach back and grab the ball. He tucked it under his arm and turned back in the right direction, all in the same motion—and then Chuck Bednarik hit him like a lifetime supply of bad news.

Thirty-three years later there are still people reeling from the Tackle, none of them named Gifford or Bednarik. In New York somebody always seems to be coming up to old number 16 of the Giants and telling him they were there the day he got starched in the Polo Grounds. (It was Yankee Stadium.) Other times they say that everything could have been avoided if Charlie Conerly had thrown the ball where he was supposed to. (George Shaw was the guilty Giant quarterback.) And then there was Howard Cosell, who sat beside Gifford on *Monday Night Football* for 14 years and seemed to bring up Bednarik whenever he was stuck for something to say. One week Cosell would accuse Bednarik of blindsiding Gifford, the next he would blame Bednarik for knocking Gifford out of football. Both were classic examples of telling it like it wasn't. But it is too late to undo any of the above, for the Tackle has taken on a life of its own. So Gifford plays along by telling what sounds like an apocryphal story about one of his early dates with the woman who would become his third wife. "Kathie Lee," he told her, "one word you're going to hear a lot of around me is Bednarik." And Kathie Lee supposedly said, "What's that, a pasta?"

For all the laughing Gifford does when he spins that yarn, there was nothing funny about Nov. 20, 1960, the day Bednarik handed him his lunch. The Eagles, who complemented Concrete Charlie and Hall of Fame quarterback Norm Van Brocklin with a roster full of tough, resourceful John Does, blew into New York intent on knocking the Giants on their media-fed reputation.

Philadelphia was leading 17–10 with under two minutes to play, but the Giants kept slashing and pounding, smelling one of those comeback victories that were supposed to be the Eagles' specialty. Then Gifford caught that pass. "I ran through him right up here," Bednarik says, slapping himself on the chest hard enough to break something. "*Right here.*" And this time he pops a visiting reporter on the chest. "It was like when you hit a home run; you say, 'Jeez, I didn't even feel it hit the bat.' "

Giants linebacker Sam Huff would later call it "the greatest tackle I've ever seen," but at the time it happened Huff's emotion was utter despair. Gifford fell backward, the ball flew forward. When Eagles linebacker Chuck Weber pounced on it, Bednarik started dancing as if St. Vitus had taken possession of him. And as he danced, he yelled at Gifford, "This game is over!" But Gifford couldn't hear him. "He didn't hurt me," Gifford insists. "When he hit me, I landed on my ass and then my head snapped back. That was what put me out—the whiplash, not Bednarik." Whatever the cause, Gifford looked like he was past tense as he lay there motionless. A funereal silence fell over the crowd, and Bednarik rejoiced no more. He has never been given to regret, but in that moment he almost changed his ways. Maybe he actually would have repented if he had been next to the first Mrs. Gifford after her husband had been carried off on a stretcher. She was standing outside the Giants' dressing room when the team physician stuck his head out the door and said, "I'm afraid he's dead." Only after she stopped wobbling did Mrs. Gifford learn that the doctor was talking about a security guard who had suffered a heart attack during the game.

Even so, Gifford didn't get off lightly. He had a concussion that kept him out for the rest of the season and all of 1961. But in '62 he returned as a flanker and played with honor for three more seasons. He would also have the good grace to invite Bednarik to play golf with him, and he would never, ever whine about the Tackle. "It was perfectly legal," Gifford says. "If I'd had the chance, I would have done the same thing to Chuck." . . .

BEDNARIK knocked Gifford out of the game . . . and the following season.

1994 | DAN MARINO had to contend with the Patriots' rush and a ravaged field in Miami | *Photograph by* GEORGE TIEDEMANN

> Artifacts

Cardboard Heroes

Beginning with college stars in the 1890s, football players have been featured on trading cards—including these from the NFL of the 1940s, '50s and '60s—encouraging little boys to dream big

WALTER "Piggy" BARNES

JULES RYKOVICH

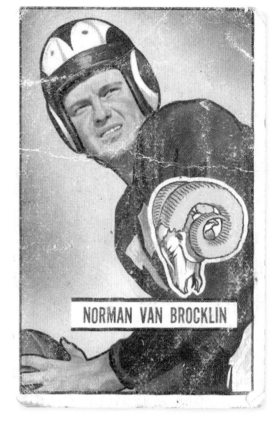

NORMAN VAN BROCKLIN

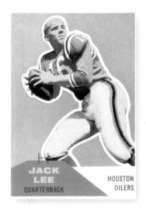

JACK LEE · QUARTERBACK · HOUSTON OILERS

ED QUIRK

KANSAS CITY · E. J. HOLUB · linebacker

JACK SPIKES · FULLBACK · DALLAS TEXANS

NEW YORK · MATT SNELL · fullback

Packers · FLOYD "Breezy" REID

PETE PIHOS

OAKLAND · JIM OTTO · center

BILL WIGHTKIN

DAN EDWARDS

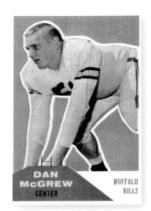

DAN McGREW
CENTER
BUFFALO BILLS

GEORGE CONNOR

THURMAN MC GRAW

BILLY KINARD
HALFBACK
BUFFALO BILLS

DON MAYNARD
NEW YORK JETS
FLANKER

BUFFALO
PAUL MAGUIRE linebacker

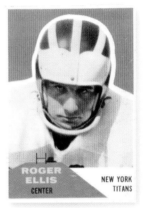

ROGER ELLIS
CENTER
NEW YORK TITANS

BILL DUDLEY

DOAK WALKER

SAN DIEGO
RON MIX tackle

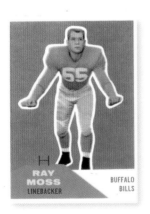

RAY MOSS
LINEBACKER
BUFFALO BILLS

BUFFALO
JACK KEMP quarterback

TOM DIMITROFF
QUARTERBACK
NEW YORK TITANS

from TOM LANDRY 1924–2000

BY PAUL ZIMMERMAN | *SI, February 21, 2000*

I T IS AN ENDURING IMAGE: THE MAN STOICALLY standing on the Dallas Cowboys sideline in his trademark hat. But when Tom Landry died of leukemia at 75, he was remembered for much more than that. Landry was a New York favorite before he ever put X's and O's to paper. In 1949 he played left cornerback—defensive halfback, as it was called in those days—for the Brooklyn–New York Yankees of the old All-America Conference, and he played the position with a roughneck style that the fans loved. Picture an early-day Mel Blount, and you've got Landry.

A year later folks around the NFL learned that there was a brain to go with the muscle. Landry played that season for the Giants, who were coached by Steve Owen. After watching the Browns, New York's next opponent, annihilate the defending champion Eagles in Philadelphia, Owen returned with a new defensive formation that he had devised, the 4–3. Landry, then 26, was the man he chose to break down the scheme on the blackboard for the team. "He can explain it better than I can," Owen said. New York shut down Cleveland's high-powered attack in a 6–0 win. The 4–3 remains the NFL's standard defensive set.

Six years later, in 1956, Landry coached the defense and Vince Lombardi oversaw the offense, giving the NFL champion Giants the most dynamic pair of assistant coaches ever to grace one staff. A visitor to the Giants that season described a walk down the corridor where the coaches' offices were located. "The first office I passed belonged to Landry," he said. "He was busy putting in a defense, running his projector, studying film. The next office was Vince Lombardi's. He was breaking down his own film, putting in an offense. The next office was head coach Jim Lee Howell's. He had his feet up on the desk, and he was reading a newspaper." Upon seeing the visitor, Howell quipped, "With guys like Lombardi and Landry in the building, there isn't much for me to do around here."

Landry would go on to build the Cowboys from an undermanned expansion team into an NFL power, first with a stunning array of offensive formations and maneuvers, then with a solid organizational structure. Perhaps the most unusual thing about Landry's early years in Dallas was that he devised both an offense and defense for his expansion babies. "I realized that I couldn't beat anyone with my personnel," he told me. "So I had to do it with the motion and formations and gadget plays—the kind of stuff that bothered me most when I was a defensive coach." The result in 1962, the team's third season, was an offense that finished second in the NFL in total yards.

In 29 seasons under Landry, Dallas won two Super Bowls, played in three other title games and went 20 consecutive years with a winning record. He ranks third in career NFL victories, with 270. In his 40-year pro career Landry was vital in forging a brand of football that the NFL could hang its hat on. . . .

1979 | THE IMAGE of a franchise for three decades, Landry stalked the sideline in his trademark fedora, under which he stolidly concealed one of the game's most inventive minds. | *Photograph by* DAVID BURNETT

2005 | BOLTING INTO the open against the Chargers, Dallas receiver Keyshawn Johnson (19) prepared to hit paydirt | *Photograph by* JOHN W. MCDONOUGH

2007 | WITH HIS third interception of the first half, San Diego's Antonio Cromartie single-handedly foiled Colts wideout Reggie Wayne | *Photograph by* CHRIS PARK

> **SI's TOP 25** *The Running Backs*

EARL CAMPBELL
Photograph by HEINZ KLUETMEIER

BRONKO NAGURSKI
Photograph by AP

FRANCO HARRIS
Photograph by JOHN IACONO

HUGH McELHENNY
Photograph by CAL PICTURES

ERIC DICKERSON
Photograph by RONALD C. MODRA

GALE SAYERS
Photograph by KEN REGAN

TONY DORSETT
Photograph by AL MESSERSCHMIDT

O.J. SIMPSON
Photograph by ERIC SCHWEIKARDT

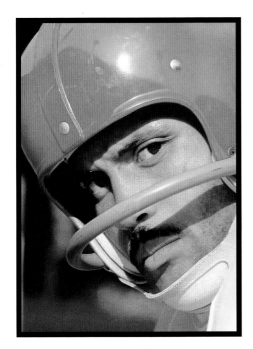

OLLIE MATSON
Photograph by JOHN G. ZIMMERMAN

MARSHALL FAULK
Photograph by TODD ROSENBERG

MARCUS ALLEN

JEROME BETTIS

JIM BROWN

EARL CAMPBELL

LARRY CSONKA

ERIC DICKERSON

TONY DORSETT

MARSHALL FAULK

RED GRANGE

FRANCO HARRIS

EDGERRIN JAMES

CURTIS MARTIN

OLLIE MATSON

HUGH MCELHENNY

MARION MOTLEY

BRONKO NAGURSKI

ERNIE NEVERS

WALTER PAYTON

BARRY SANDERS

GALE SAYERS

O.J. SIMPSON

EMMITT SMITH

JIM TAYLOR

JIM THORPE

LADAINIAN TOMLINSON

THE LION KING

BY PAUL ZIMMERMAN

Barry Sanders ran circles around NFL defenses with an electrifying style unlike anything the league had seen

— *from* SI, DECEMBER 8, 1997

BARRY SANDERS IS WHAT people in the NFL call a "freak runner." Defensive coaches can't draw up a scheme to stop him because his style follows no predictable pattern. It's all improvisation, genius, eyes that see more than other people's do, legs that seem to operate as disjointed entities, intuition, awareness of where the danger is—all performed in a churning, thrashing heartbeat.

The coaches will say things like "surround him," "cut off his escape angles" and "make sure you maintain your backside lanes," all the stuff they have been preaching since the days of Red Grange. For a while this might work, and there will be a neat little collection of one- and minus-two-yard runs in Sanders's pile. Then perhaps someone will get a little tired or misjudge an angle, and it's *whoosh*, there he goes!

It doesn't matter where the play is blocked; he'll find his own soft spot. It doesn't matter if he's running with a fullback in front of him or from a double-tight-end set or out of the old three- and four-wideout Silver Streak offense that the Detroit Lions used to employ. "What a waste," we used to say. "Four wideouts and Barry. Give him a fullback like Moose Johnston, put him behind a Dallas-caliber All Pro line, and he'd get his double G-note in yardage every season."

Well, this year the Lions gave him a blocking fullback and a fairly conventional offense, and after Sanders ran for 53 yards on 25 carries in his first two games, we all said, "Look what they've done. They've ruined him." Since then he has reeled off 11 straight games of 100 yards or more rushing.

The point is, the scheme doesn't seem to matter with Sanders. He can run from any alignment. While other people are stuck with joints, he seems to have ball bearings in his legs that give him a mechanical advantage. But there are drawbacks: He's not a goal line or short-yardage runner, though he's staying in the game more than he used to in those situations. When you need someone to smack in there for a tough yard, you can't take a chance with a guy who can lose three as easily as he gains 30. (During his nine-year career, he has been dumped for losses on 336 carries, almost 14% of his total rushing attempts, for 952 yards.) For this reason I believe he is behind Jim Brown on the alltime list of great running backs. Brown had that extra dimension of short-yardage muscle.

When you look at some of the great runners of the past— Grange, Bill Dudley, Ollie Matson, Gale Sayers—that's what you see, great running through a broken field, a field in which there's space to maneuver. Sanders's finest runs often occur when he takes the handoff and, with a couple of moves, turns the line of scrimmage into a broken field. Walter Payton ran with fury and attacked tacklers. O.J. Simpson and Eric Dickerson were instinctive runners who glided into the line and sliced through it with a burst, but nobody has ever created such turmoil at the point of attack as Sanders has.

Freak runners usually burn out quickly. One injury, one glitch in the stop-and-start mechanism, and the whole equation breaks down. But Sanders has missed only seven games because of injury, one in his rookie season, one in 1991 and five in '93. Knock on wood, he seems indestructible. . . .

SANDERS WAS just 1,457 yards short of Walter Payton's NFL career rushing record when he walked away from the Lions in 1998.

1976 | MEAN JOE GREENE of Pittsburgh (75) drew a bead on Oakland's Mark van Eeghen during the AFC Championship Game won by the Raiders | *Photograph by* NEIL LEIFER

1967 | GLAD-HANDING COACH George Allen celebrated with Diron Talbert (72) and Billy Truax after Los Angeles edged the Packers | *Photograph by* NEIL LEIFER

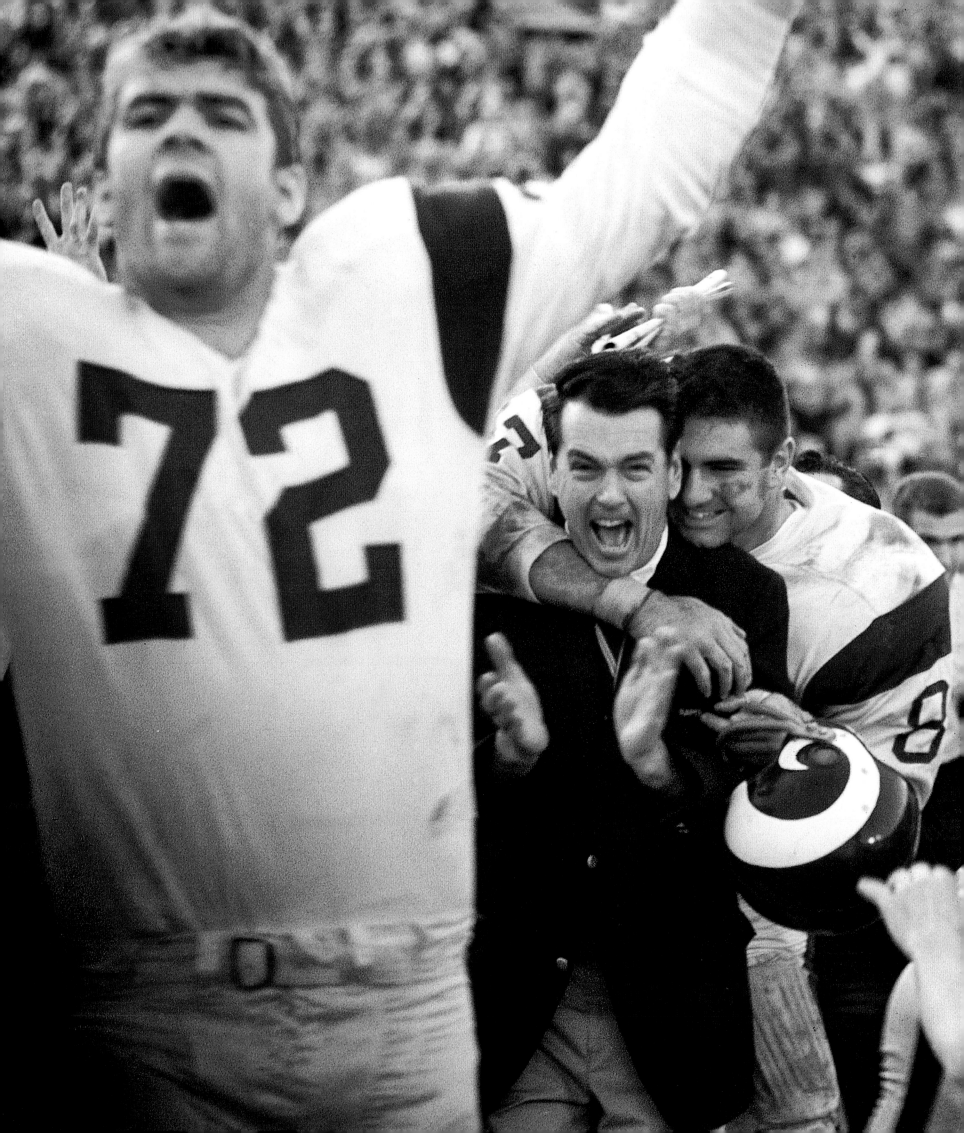

1962 | **THE GIANTS** didn't need anyone to light a fire under them for a December game against Green Bay in Yankee Stadium | *Photograph by* NEIL LEIFER

HEY T.O., ARE YOU READY FOR SOME FOOTBALL?

BY KARL TARO GREENFELD

After Terrell Owens burned his bridges behind him, he was contrite (well, a little), happy and hungry to win with the Cowboys. —*from* SI, JULY 24, 2006

WHEN TERRELL OWENS SMILES, you expect a mischievous upturn of the lips, but instead he flashes a broad grin full of bright teeth and uncomplicated joy. You anticipate villainy—years of bad press have had their effect—but what Owens shows right now is only satisfaction at joining the Cowboys and giddiness at the prospect of imminent revenge. Owens might be the most universally reviled supremely talented athlete of his era (at least Barry Bonds is beloved in San Francisco), having assumed that mantle at some point during his four-month broken-field run through the sports news cycle last summer and fall. The controversial touchdown celebrations for which he became famous now seem quaint after his immolation of the Philadelphia Eagles' 2005 season. There were days last year when ESPN seemed to be TOPN, constantly airing interviews with Owens and his agent, Drew Rosenhaus, following his comings and goings from training camp and his meetings with coaches and team executives, Sal Paolantonio doing stand-ups in front of the Eagles' NovaCare Complex, looking as stern and concerned as if he were covering an unfolding hostage situation.

In a sense, that's precisely what it was: a star player holding a team hostage. Owens and Rosenhaus, of course, will lecture you on the unfairness of NFL contracts, asserting that the Eagles (who had signed Owens in March 2004 to a seven-year, $49 million contract, only $2.3 million of which was guaranteed) had no intention of paying Owens's $7 million roster bonus for '06, and that T.O.'s cause—to ensure that he was one of the best-paid receivers in the league—was just. (Entering the '05 season he wasn't even in the top 10 if signing bonuses are included.) But even if you take the position that in America a man has a right to demand as much cheddar as he wants, you have to wonder at the methods Owens used to make his case: Being sent home for a week after feuding with his coach and offensive coordinator at training camp, then performing crunches in front of his New Jersey home on national television, was perhaps not the most persuasive negotiating strategy. And dissing his quarterback, Donovan McNabb, in an interview that ended up splashed all over ESPN was the surest way to lose those few remaining fans still in his camp.

It was almost enough to make you forget what Owens had accomplished on the field. Actually, it probably was enough to make you forget, so let's review: If T.O. had left the NovaCare Complex after his suspension by the Eagles in early November and never played again, you could easily make the case that he still belonged in the Hall of Fame: In 10 seasons he had 716 catches, more than 10,000 yards receiving and 101 touchdowns, fourth most in NFL history. Owens holds the single-game reception record (20, San Francisco versus Chicago, Dec. 17, 2000), was named to five straight Pro Bowls from '00 to '04, turned in five straight 1,000-yard seasons and delivered riveting moments in big games: splitting two Packers for a game-winning touchdown catch in a January 1999 playoff game; coming back from a broken leg and sprained ankle to turn in an MVP-worthy performance in the 2004 Super Bowl. (And as any aficionado of *Madden NFL* will tell you, there has never been a better third-and-seven receiver in the history of computer games.)

Now he's a Cowboy. His off-season move from Philadelphia, which released him on March 14, to Dallas, with whom he signed a three-year, $25 million contract later that month, has made the Cowboys a fashionable preseason Super Bowl pick and Drew Bledsoe the happiest quarterback in Texas. Bledsoe believes that Owens's ability to draw double teams far outweighs his baggage.

"What's past is past," says Bledsoe. "He's an explosive, powerful receiver who runs good routes and catches the ball well. . . . His impact is going to be felt not only in his production but also in the production of the other people on the field."

That sentiment was expressed more directly in the text message Bledsoe sent to Owens after their minicamp in May, "This year is gonna be sick.". . .

OWENS'S SUPREME talent has outweighed his tendency to disrupt his teams, and that puts him a step ahead of Pacman Jones (32).

1998 | DOLPHINS CORNERBACK Jerry Wilson made a splash after taking down Pittsburgh running back Fred McAfee | *Photograph* BY BILL FRAKES

2004 | THE TRACK was rated sloppy in Foxborough (opposite), and so was the uniform of New England linebacker Justin Kurpeikis | *Photograph by* EZRA SHAW

Ball and Change

The old pigskin has varied in size, shape and even color, but there's always been one constant: funny bounces

c. 1895 | Oldest ball in the Pro Football Hall of Fame

1911 | Game ball used by
Columbus Panhandles, an early pro team

1935 | Ball used in championship game
and signed by the winners, the Detroit Lions

c. 1950 | White balls were approved
for use in NFL games from 1931 until 1953

1958 | Sudden-death championship game ball
from Baltimore Colts' win over New York Giants

1967 | Game ball used on offense in
Super Bowl I by the AFL team, the Chiefs

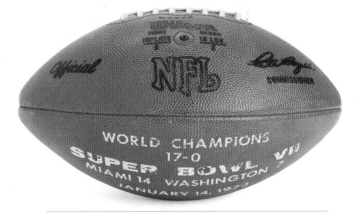

1973 | Ball used in Super Bowl VII
to complete the Dolphins' 17–0 season

THE LAST ANGRY MEN

BY RICK TELANDER

Running backs beware: All the best linebackers play with a chip on their shoulders. — *from* SI, SEPTEMBER 6, 1993

LINEBACKERS RISE OUT of the football ooze in a curious twist on Darwin: While the primitive stayed below, groveling on all fours, the *more* primitive ascended to the upright position. Of course in the beginning there were no linebackers at all in football. Because there was no forward pass, there was no need on defense for anything other than seven or eight down linemen who rooted like pigs and three or four defensive backs who could run down any ballcarrier who got past the swine. With the dawn of the pass in professional football in 1906, defensive principles slowly evolved. "Roving centers" started to pop up, and by 1920 something like a modern-day NFL middle linebacker had emerged. His name was George Trafton, and he played for the Decatur Staleys, who became the Bears. There is some dispute as to whether Trafton was the first true linebacker, but he was definitely the first Butkus-like personality in the NFL. Nicknamed the Brute, Trafton was as nasty as they come, despised by rival teams and their fans. In a Rock Island (Ill.) *Argus* account of a Staley game in 1920, Trafton was described as "sliding across the face of the rival center." Against the Independents in Rock Island that same year, Trafton took umbrage at a rumor that an opponent, a halfback named Fred Chicken, was out to get him. The Brute promptly knocked Chicken out with a hit that broke his leg. On the final play Staleys' coach George Halas sent Trafton running for the exit and a waiting taxi. Angry Rock Island fans mobbed the taxi, and Trafton had to hitch a ride with a passing motorist to get himself safely out of town. According to Bob Carroll, the executive director of the Professional Football Researchers Association, the first outside linebacker in the NFL was 6' 4" John Alexander, who played for the Milwaukee Badgers. Normally a tackle, one day in 1922 Alexander "stood up, took a step back, two steps out and became an outside linebacker," says Carroll. "He wondered why, as tall as he was, he was always getting down on the ground where he couldn't see." Alexander set the evolutionary clock moving, and 60 years later it brought us to LT.

Some people think that modern outside linebackers, blitz specialists primarily, aren't really linebackers at all, but gussied-up defensive ends. Some people say that inside linebackers, whether in tandem in a 3–4 alignment or standing alone in the increasingly rare 4–3 (wasn't a big part of Dick Butkus's dark majesty that aloneness?), are the only true linebackers today. But linebacking is really about responsibilities and attitude, not formations. Pain is the thing that separates linebackers from everyone else on the field—both dishing it out and receiving it. Linebackers dish out pain because it intimidates opponents. Says Butkus, "In college I figured punishing the ballcarrier wouldn't intimidate anybody, but it did. Then, in the pros, I thought I'd meet guys like me, but there were still guys who were chickens---, guys with big yellow streaks."

Linebackers see the game as superseding all guidelines on basic empathy for one's fellow man. "You want to punish the running backs," says Steelers Pro Bowl linebacker Greg Lloyd. "You like to kick them and, when they get down, kick them again. Until they wave the white flag." Or as Sam Huff of the Giants said to TIME magazine in 1959, "We try to hurt everybody."

Even themselves at times. The euphoria that linebackers experience afield comes during the white flash of great collisions—enlightenment literally being a blow to the head. Lloyd split two blockers in a game against the Cleveland Browns last year and then met runner Kevin Mack head-on. The ensuing crash overwhelmed Lloyd. "I was dizzy, my head was hurting and my eyes were watering," he says. "It felt good."

Where does such lunacy come from? "Off the field I'm quiet, laid-back, relaxed," says Eagles star Seth Joyner. "On the field I talk all kinds of garbage. I think it's a way to vent your anger."

Anger over what? Butkus struggles with the question. It's not really anger, he says. It's more a desire to set things right, to prove, as he says, "you don't get something for nothing." Violence can resolve ambivalence and uncertainty. And who doesn't crave certainty in life, a reward for the good, punishment for the bad? Things are so simple when you're a linebacker. One afternoon while Butkus was practicing with his high school team, he noticed four boys in a car harassing his girlfriend, Helen Essenberg, who was across the street. Without hesitation Butkus ran off the field, chased the car, dived through the open front window on the passenger side and, in full uniform, thrashed each of the passengers. Then he climbed out of the car and walked back to the field. He never said a word to Helen, who is now his wife. He had done what needed to be done, and it was over. "They could have been her friends, for all I knew," he says. . . .

RAY NITSCHKE was, according to Bart Starr, a "classic" Jekyll and Hyde type—a sweetheart off the field, a savage demon on it.

2004 | TIPTOEING ALONG the sideline, Pittsburgh's Antwaan Randle El (82) shrugged off the Redskins' Marcus Washington | *Photograph by* RICK STEWART

2005 | NEW ENGLAND'S Deion Branch (83) clearly had both feet inbounds before impact by the Eagles' Michael Lewis in Super Bowl XXXIX | *Photograph by* HEINZ KLUETMEIER

HONOR GUARD

BY GARY SMITH

True to his legacy as one of the game's greatest offensive linemen, all-powerful union chief Gene Upshaw blocked out any hint of his mortality until the end. —*from* SI, SEPTEMBER 1, 2008

O F COURSE, DEATH COULD have him as it could have any man: any way it wanted. But an odd thing happened last week once it entered that big house, Gene Upshaw. Death *became* him. Secretive. Abrupt. Adamant. Accidents and heart attacks have whisked major sports figures off the stage more suddenly, but has disease ever taken one with such swiftness and stealth?

As stunned as his loved ones, friends, colleagues and adversaries were, they recognized death's eerie mimicry of his life. Some remembered those Saturday nights at his dinner table, talking and laughing over coffee and tequila, when the NFL legend would go off to do the dishes, return and announce that the party was over—then turn out the lights. Others had been at the negotiating table with him when he smelled something foul, fell silent, arose and walked out. When Gene Upshaw decided it was time to go, he went. He didn't say goodbye.

He went last Wednesday, August 20, in the ICU at Tahoe Forest Hospital. Paul Tagliabue, the former NFL commissioner and friend who'd partnered with Upshaw to restructure the league's economics and usher in an era of fantastic wealth, issued a statement hours later declaring that few players in history had had Upshaw's impact on the NFL. "And I sat there all day thinking, Who else is in that few?" said Tagliabue. "I didn't want to say no one else has ever had that impact. But it may be no one."

Tagliabue hadn't seen Upshaw in a few months, but he'd heard the whispers. Weight was melting off the big man who'd ruled the NFL Players Association for a quarter century. Plenty of people were pointing it out to Gene. But he'd just shrug it off, and their acquaintance with Upshaw's iron will made them hesitant to press the point. Dr. Thom Mayer, the NFLPA's medical director as well as a friend, advised him to get tests but didn't waste his breath when Gene decided to wait until after his annual family vacation. In Upshaw's Hall of Fame NFL career, 15 years of trench savagery, he never once came out of a game.

On the night of Aug. 15, a Friday, he celebrated his 63rd birthday in Tahoe, and the resonance that number held wasn't lost on him. That was the license-plate number that linebackers and cornerbacks looked up and saw rumbling away after Upshaw—a mastodon four decades ago at 6'5", 265—had flattened them as he led sweeps for perhaps the greatest offensive line in NFL history. "Number 63 turned 63," Gene kept chortling on that Friday night. Then he lay down in bed, and his breaths grew short, and the symmetry grew grim.

What kind of cancer had he contracted? By his second night in the hospital, doctors were almost certain they had I.D.'d their enemy: the most vicious of all, the one known as the silent disease, pancreatic cancer. He was moved from the ER to a hospital room at Tahoe Forest, checking in, Upshawish to the end, under an assumed name. Not a peep of his condition trickled to the media or to his home office in Washington, the skeletally staffed outfit he'd inherited in 1983. But what else was new? Upshaw was a relic executive, with little concern for p.r. and less for transparency: a sealed vault. What he hadn't learned about tight lips from his old man, Eugene Sr., he'd gotten from his next mentor, the sultan of secrecy, Raiders owner Al Davis. All these years after working his way up the NFLPA ranks—from player rep to president to executive director—Gene still fetched his own coffee, left his staff in the dark about his whereabouts and rarely answered his cellphone. "I know where I'm going, but I don't explain," he'd say. "If you're too open, then everyone will find something wrong with everything. They'll get a finger in the pie."

That got him into trouble, deep trouble, with a group of loud retired players who didn't like their slice of the disability and pension pies and didn't like Gene's slice—with bonuses, Upshaw's 2006 income was reported as $6.7 million. It landed him in front of a congressional hearing last September and landed him in a media firestorm. And maybe even, those who could only imagine the stress he'd swallowed over the last two years might wonder, landed him here at Tahoe Forest with a gutful of cancer.

The disease advanced with shocking speed. There went the kidneys. Then the liver. Then the heart. Just like that. The only man to play in Super Bowls in three decades, to start in championship games in the AFL and the NFL. The most influential black labor leader in America and the only athlete to later take the reins of his sport's union. Gone.

Once he got the word, said Dr. Mayer, it was as if he'd drawn up a game plan, "and said, 'This is how a man dies.'" . . .

AS AN 11-time All-Pro and an iron-gripped leader of the players union, Upshaw was the epitome of power—until his shockingly swift end.

1988 | THERE WAS agony for Redskins QB Doug Williams in the first quarter of
Super Bowl XXII but ecstasy when he returned to earn the game's MVP | *Photograph by* JOHN BIEVER

> ## SI's TOP 25 *The Receivers*

DON HUTSON
Photograph by AP

JERRY RICE
Photograph by ALLEN KEE

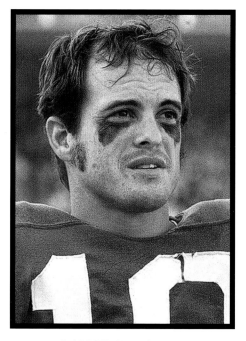

LANCE ALWORTH
Photograph by JOHN G. ZIMMERMAN

KELLEN WINSLOW
Photograph by PETER READ MILLER

CRIS CARTER
Photograph by TOM DIPACE

PAUL WARFIELD
Photograph by TONY TOMSIC

LYNN SWANN
Photograph by AP

FRED BILETNIKOFF
Photograph by RICH CLARKSON

SHANNON SHARPE
Photograph by ALBERT DICKSON

MARVIN HARRISON
Photograph by TOM DIPACE

LANCE ALWORTH

RAYMOND BERRY

FRED BILETNIKOFF

TIM BROWN

CRIS CARTER

MIKE DITKA

TONY GONZALEZ

MARVIN HARRISON

ELROY (CRAZY LEGS) HIRSCH

DON HUTSON

CHARLIE JOINER

STEVE LARGENT

DANTE LAVELLI

JOHN MACKEY

DON MAYNARD

BOBBY MITCHELL

RANDY MOSS

OZZIE NEWSOME

TERRELL OWENS

JERRY RICE

SHANNON SHARPE

LYNN SWANN

CHARLEY TAYLOR

PAUL WARFIELD

KELLEN WINSLOW

THEY'RE HISTORY!

BY TIM LAYDEN

Thanks to a ferocious defense and a miraculous drive, the Giants pulled off one of the NFL's great upsets, knocking off the unbeaten Patriots in Super Bowl XLII. —*from* SI, FEBRUARY 11, 2008

THIS TIME THE CELEBRATION was for the youngest child of a football family, and for the team he helped carry to an unlikely championship. A year ago in Miami, Eli Manning had seen his older brother Peyton transformed by a Super Bowl championship. He had seen Peyton walk into his own victory party so blissfully satisfied that the moment found a place in Eli's soul and changed him as well. "It put a hunger inside me," Eli says. "You always want to win, but after that I felt like I wanted it even more." And now, so soon afterward, it would be his turn.

A second-floor restaurant at the New York Giants' team hotel outside Phoenix had become a thrumming nightclub into early Monday morning, a steady bass beat beneath the unmistakable buzz of victory at another Manning Super Bowl celebration. It was to have been a historic night. The New England Patriots would win their 19th consecutive game and become only the second NFL team, along with the 1972 Miami Dolphins, to complete a season unbeaten and untied. They would fortify the legacy of a modern professional dynasty with a fourth Super Bowl title in seven years. They would prove themselves perfect. Instead, the Giants completed an unexpected and emotional postseason run with a 17–14 victory in a game that will take its place as the second-greatest upset in a Super Bowl, behind the New York Jets' epic 16–7 defeat of the Baltimore Colts in January '69.

This Super Bowl would be either a coronation or a colossal upset. The Patriots had spent the entirety of their 16–0 regular season and their run through the AFC playoffs denying their pursuit of history, but that larger task defined the game. The Giants, who were 10–6 in the regular season and the fifth seed in the NFC playoffs, slowly grew sick of their role. "Everywhere you went," said cornerback R.W. McQuarters, "it was all about the Patriots and 19–0." On Sunday, they redefined it.

Mixing A-gap blitzes from weakside linebacker Kawika Mitchell with steady four-man pressure from the line, the Giants brought relentless heat to Patriots quarterback Tom Brady and the highest-scoring offense in NFL history. New York had five sacks and knocked Brady down a half-dozen other times. The upshot of all this defense—New England's unit also played solidly—was a brutal game in which, after the Patriots took a 7–3 lead on the first play of the second quarter, the two teams went 33 minutes, 52 seconds without scoring, a Super Bowl record. Then they played a 15-minute masterpiece, compressing a night's drama into the fourth quarter.

First, Manning threw a touchdown pass to David Tyree with 11:05 to play. Three series later, Brady completed 8 of 11 on an 80-yard drive, capping it with a six-yard TD pass to Randy Moss that put New England back on top 14–10 with 2:42 remaining. The game rested in Manning's hands. Manning had been neither brilliant nor bad (14 of 25 for 178 yards with one touchdown and one interception) when he took the field for what would be the defining drive of his career. The Giants took six plays to move from their 17-yard line to their 44, where, on third-and-five, Manning took a shotgun snap and carved a place in football lore. Quickly swarmed in a collapsing pocket, he was grabbed by the Patriots' Jarvis Green, a 6'3", 285-pound defensive end. For an instant Manning disappeared, presumed sacked. Somehow, though, he pulled away from the scrum. His mother watched and was transported back nearly four decades, to a time when her sweetheart was tearing up the Southeastern Conference. Said Olivia Manning, "That looked like Archie running around at Ole Miss."

Once free, Manning squared himself and lobbed a pass into the middle of the field toward Tyree, who had stopped after running a post pattern. A fifth-year wideout best known for his special-teams work, Tyree scarcely fit the hero's mold—he had caught only four passes in the regular season and one in the playoffs. But with the Super Bowl in the balance, Tyree rose high and outfought Patriots veteran strong safety Rodney Harrison, clutching the ball against his own helmet. The 32-yard gain took the ball to the New England 24-yard line. Three plays later Manning threw 12 yards to rookie Steve Smith for a first down at the Patriots' 13 with 39 seconds left.

The Giants' next formation sent wideout Plaxico Burress to the left, and the Patriots blitzed, leaving cornerback Ellis Hobbs in single coverage on Burress. Hobbs guessed slant— "He pretty much has to guess one way or the other," said Peyton Manning—the play called for a fade, and Hobbs was badly beaten. "End of story," said Eli. . . .

STICKER SHOCK: In the game's most indelible moment, the tenacious Tyree fought off Harrison and miraculously clutched Manning's heave to his helmet.

1972 | JOE NAMATH was known for his flashy wardrobe off the field; on the field, his signature look included white shoes and a heavy knee brace that today looks medieval | *Photograph by* NEIL LEIFER *(right)*

2006 | HINES WARD was dancing on air as he scored the clinching touchdown against Seattle in Super Bowl XL | *Photograph by* JOHN W. MCDONOUGH

2006 | REGGIE BUSH tacked the finishing touch on a double reverse by sailing over the Steelers' Ryan Clark for a score | *Photograph by* MIKE EHRMANN

from FROZEN IN TIME | BY JOHNETTE HOWARD
SI January 13, 1997

T HERE WAS A TIME WHEN PRO-
fessional football franchises routinely settled in small towns
like Canton and Kenosha and Green Bay. A time when
Lambeau Field was not a quaint anomaly, when everyone
played football on grass and there were no Teflon roofs to
shut out the midday sun or hermetically sealed domes to block the winter
wind. In 1961, when coach Vince Lombardi's players hoisted him into the air
for his first NFL title ride, only God's gray sky hung overhead, just as it had
at all football games back then.

The Packers were a league power in that era, and Lambeau Field was the
NFL's answer to Boston Garden and Yankee Stadium—hallowed ground
where dynasties were born. During Lombardi's nine-year stint as coach of
the Packers, they won five league championships, including the first two
Super Bowls. And no matter how many winters have passed since then, within the magical space of Lambeau Field it still seems to be 1967. "Forget Dallas," says Fuzzy Thurston, who played guard for Green Bay from 1959 to '67.
"The Green Bay Packers are America's Team."

The more things change in the rest of pro sports, the more things remain
blissfully the same in Green Bay.

People go out of their way to stop at Lambeau, even when they have no
tickets—even when the stadium is empty. Immediately after Green Bay defeated the Carolina Panthers to take the NFC championship on Jan. 12, 1997,
the gates of the stadium were thrown open so that fans could watch the awards
ceremony. Visitors ask to be shown the spot in the south end zone where, in
the 1967 NFL championship game—the Ice Bowl—Bart Starr plunged into the
end zone from the one-yard line to give the Pack a 21–17 win over the Dallas
Cowboys. It's as if setting foot on the sacred ground gives life to the grainy
black-and-white film that shows Starr burrowing across the goal line with 13 seconds to play, his arms hugging the football in the -46° windchill as if he were protecting a newborn from the cold. "With Lombardi it was never cold here,"
says Thurston. "Before games he'd just say something like, 'Men, it's a little
blustery out there today.' Blustery, see? Then he'd say, 'It's our kind of day.
Now get out there and strut around like it's the middle of July.' " . . .

1967 | PLAYERS AND FANS at Lambeau Field endured the
-46° windchill at the Ice Bowl. | *Photograph by* BETTMANN

1971 | THE COLTS' margin of victory over the Cowboys in Super Bowl V was provided by Jim O'Brien (80) on this field goal | *Photograph by* NEIL LEIFER

1962 | THE PACKERS' grasp exceeded their reach as they tried to knock down a chip shot by 49ers kicker Tommy Davis | *Photograph by* NEIL LEIFER

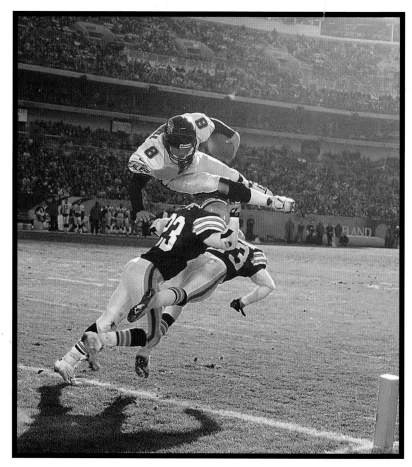

1999 | JAGUARS QUARTERBACK Mark Brunell went up (top, left) and over two Browns to reach the end zone in Cleveland | *Photographs by* JOHN BIEVER

from FURY ON THE FIELD | BY PAUL ZIMMERMAN

SI November 8, 1999

FEW NFL PLAYERS HAVE POSSESSED the fire that burned inside Walter Payton. How could this have happened to Walter Payton—a man defined by his great, passionate bursts of life? Waiting nine months for a transplant that could have saved him, slowly sinking, gradually slipping away. He played football in a frenzy, attacking tacklers with a fury that almost seemed personal. He got stronger as the game went on. Defenses tired, he attacked them.

In 1982, near the height of a remarkable career in which he rushed for more yards (16,726) than any man in history, I interviewed him at the Chicago Bears' training camp in Lake Forest, Ill. We were sitting in the lobby of the players' dorm. He had brought his motorcycle in and leaned it against a wall. Twilight was approaching but the lights in the lobby hadn't been turned on yet, and as we talked, he kept bouncing to his feet to emphasize some point—he couldn't sit still. His eyes sparkled in that half light, and I got this weird feeling that there was a glow around him, that he was giving off sparks, that there was some kind of fire burning inside, lighting him up. It was the fire of pure energy.

He told me about his off-season workouts, how he'd run up and down the steep levees near his home in Mississippi, how he'd burn out anyone foolish enough to try to keep up with him. He played in 186 straight games to finish his 13-year NFL career. All of them played at a furious pace.

"A little bundle of dynamite," Dallas Cowboys safety Cliff Harris once called him. This was after the 1977 Bears-Cowboys playoff game, and Harris, one of the more vicious hitters in NFL history, described a knockout shot he had laid on Payton. "As he caught a pass and turned upfield, I caught him just right, one of the hardest hits I ever delivered," Harris said. "He just bounced up and patted me on the behind and ran back to the huddle. I'd heard that you could never keep him on the ground. Now I know for sure."

Now, at 45, he's gone. It's hard to imagine. . . .

1981 | PAYTON WENT around, through and sometimes over the defense to pick up precious yards. | *Photograph by* RONALD C. MODRA

1962 | NOTHING WAS a snap for the diminutive Cowboys quarterback Eddie LeBaron, not even the Cardinals | *Photograph by* MARVIN E. NEWMAN

THE DAY WORLD WAR II KICKED OFF

BY S.L. PRICE

On Dec. 7, 1941, the Redskins and the Eagles played football, not knowing that the U.S. had joined the rest of the world at war.
—*from* SI, NOVEMBER 29, 1999

EVERYONE IN WASHINGton, D.C.'s Griffith Stadium that day knew his role. The wives walked in together, chattering like a flock of birds. The 27,102 fans shoved through the turnstiles, ready to shout and clap, to watch and feel. The press box filled with reporters prepared to scribble their notes. On the field the players tried to keep warm. Some were stars, some weren't. It was the final pro football game of the season for the Washington Redskins and the Philadelphia Eagles. It was quite cold. People stamped their feet. They could see their breath.

Kickoff was at 2 p.m. — 9 a.m. in Hawaii. Bombs had already fallen on the U.S. fleet, men had died, war had come. In the stands, no one knew: The game was still everything. Philadelphia had taken a 7–0 lead on its first drive. Announcements began to pour out of the P.A. system. *Admiral Bland is asked to report to his office. . . . Captain H.X. Fenn is asked to report. . . . The resident commissioner of the Philippines is urged to report. . . .* "We didn't know what the hell was going on," says Sammy Baugh, the Redskins' quarterback that day. "I had never heard that many announcements one right after another. We felt something was up, but we just kept playing."

Only the boys in the press box had any idea. Just before kickoff an Associated Press reporter named Pat O'Brien got a message ordering him to keep his story short. When O'Brien complained, another message flashed: *The Japanese have kicked off. War now!* But Redskins president George Marshall wouldn't allow an announcement of Japan's attack during the game, explaining that it would distract the fans. That made Griffith Stadium one of the last outposts of an era that had already slipped away.

The crowd oohed and cheered. When the game—and season—ended with Washington a 20–14 winner, a few hundred fans rushed the goalposts. No one took much notice of Eagles rookie halfback Nick Basca. He hadn't played much all year, making his mark mostly as a kicker and punter, and on this day he'd converted just two extra points. Baugh, with three touchdown passes, was the game's hero.

Then everyone walked out of the stadium: the wives, the future Hall of Famer, the crowd. Outside, newsboys hawked the news. The world tilted; football lost all importance; roles shifted. Women began fearing for their men. Reporters and fans would be soldiers soon. The world would not be divided into players and spectators again for a very long time. "Everybody could feel it," Baugh says.

Baugh went home to Texas and waited for a call from his draft board that never came; he was granted a deferment to stay on his ranch and raise beef cattle. During the war he flew in on the weekends for games.

Nick Basca, meanwhile, had played his final game. A native of tiny Phoenixville, Pa., and a standout at Villanova, Basca enlisted in the Army three days after Pearl Harbor with his younger brother Stephen, who left Europe with three Purple Hearts. Nick was piloting a tank in Gen. George Patton's celebrated Fourth Armored Division in France when, on Nov. 11, 1944, the tank hit a mine and was blown apart.

In later years no one talked much about Nick's short pro football career. Then, in 1991, 50 years after events had rendered it meaningless, that game between Philadelphia and Washington became everything again. Stephen Basca Jr. says, "My father was lying 60 miles away in a hospital bed when Nick was killed. They recorded on his chart that he had gotten up screaming about the time Nick's tank blew up. [In 1991] my father and I were sitting watching TV, and they showed a clip of that old game. My dad froze in his chair. It was the first time I'd ever seen him cry." . . .

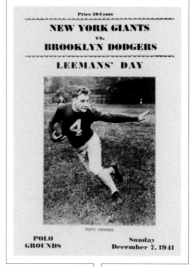

Price 10 Cents

NEW YORK GIANTS
vs.
BROOKLYN DODGERS

LEEMANS' DAY

TUFFY LEEMANS

POLO GROUNDS

Sunday December 7, 1941

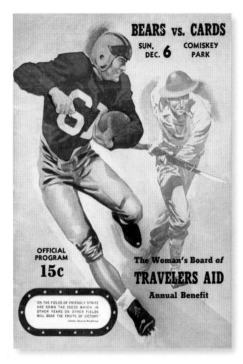

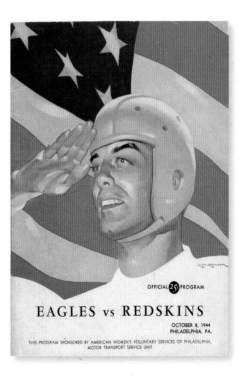

THE PATRIOTISM of the war years was reflected on NFL programs after news of Pearl Harbor spread on that December Sunday *(opposite)*.

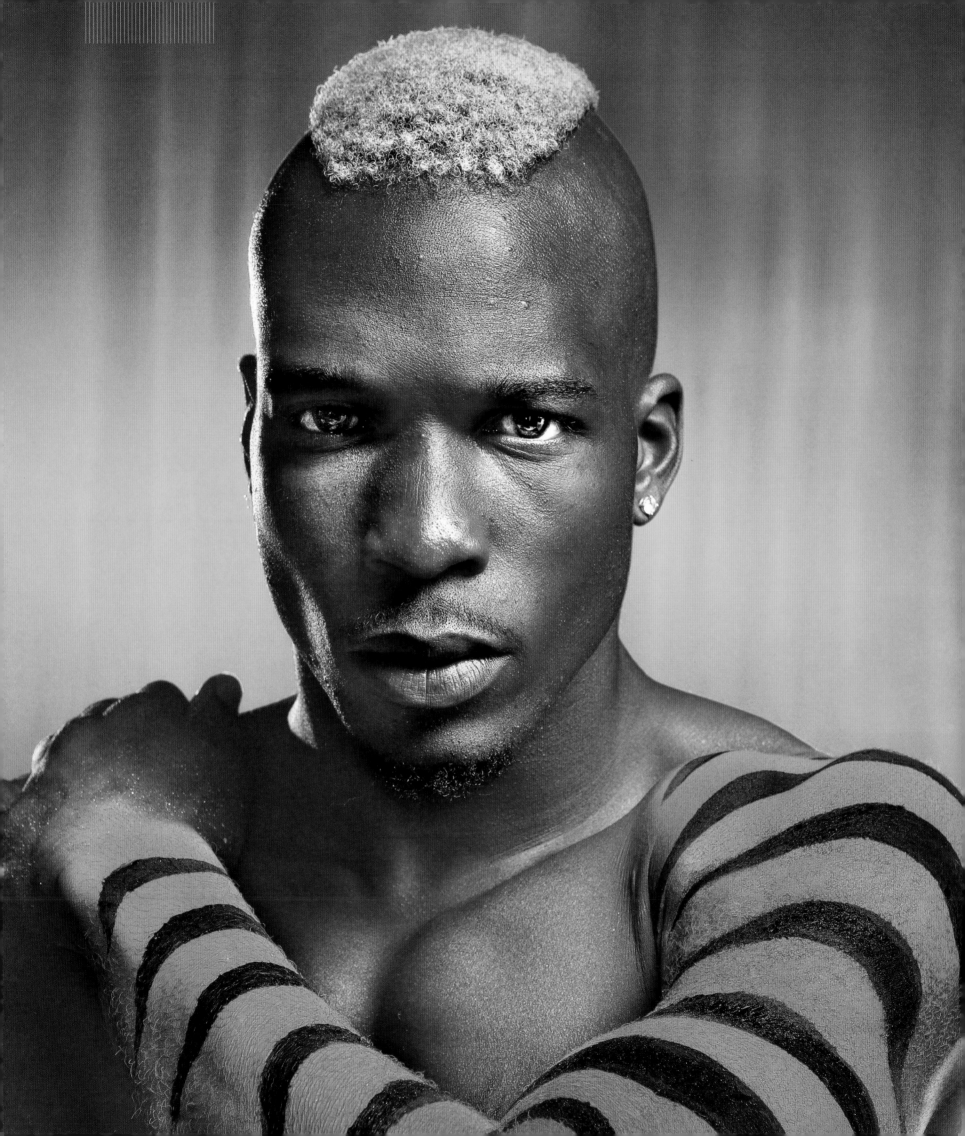

2006 | IN ADDITION to his amazing athleticism, Chad Johnson evinced an artistic streak and perhaps a hint of irreverence | *Photograph by* MICHAEL J. LEBRECHT II

2006 | OPPOSING OFFENSES didn't have a prayer when Ravens linebacker Ray Lewis, twice Defensive Player of the Year, suited up | *Photograph by* MICHAEL O'NEILL

1962 | THE BROWNS Bernie Parrish climbed the ladder on an extra-point attempt by the Giants in Cleveland | *Photograph by* TONY TOMSIC

THE BEST THERE EVER WAS

BY FRANK DEFORD

Johnny Unitas was more than just a boyhood hero for a Baltimore native. He was an inspiration for the entire city.
—*from* SI, SEPTEMBER 23, 2002

SOMETIMES, EVEN IF IT WAS only yesterday, or even if it just feels like it was only yesterday. . . . Sometimes, no matter how detailed the historical accounts, no matter how many the eyewitnesses, no matter how complete the statistics, no matter how vivid the film. . . . Sometimes, I'm sorry, but. . . . Sometimes, you just had to be there. That was the way it was with Johnny Unitas in the prime of his life, when he played for the Baltimore Colts and changed a team and a city and a league. Johnny U was an American original, a piece of work like none other, excepting maybe Paul Bunyan or Horatio Alger.

Part of it was that he came out of nowhere, like Athena springing forth full-grown from the brow of Zeus, or like Shoeless Joe Hardy from Hannibal, Mo., magically joining the Senators, compliments of the devil. But that was myth, and that was fiction. Johnny U was real, before our eyes.

Nowadays, of course, flesh peddlers and scouting services identify the best athletes when they are still in junior high. Prospects are not allowed to sneak up on us. But back then, 1956, was a quaint time when we still could be pleasantly surprised. Unitas just surfaced there on the roster, showing up one day after a tryout. The new number 19 was identified as "YOU-ni-tass" when he first appeared in an exhibition, and only later did we learn that he had played, somewhere between obscurity and anonymity, at Louisville and then, for six bucks a game, on the dusty Pittsburgh sandlots. His was a story out of legend, if not, indeed, out of religious tradition: the unlikely savior come out of nowhere.

The quarterback for the Colts then was George Shaw, the very first pick in the NFL draft the year before, the man ordained to lead a team that was coalescing into a contender. Didn't we wish, in Baltimore! Didn't we dream! The Colts had Alan (the Horse) Ameche and Lenny (Spats) Moore and L.G. (Long Gone) Dupre to carry the ball and Raymond Berry and

Jim Mutscheller to catch it and Artie Donovan and Big Daddy Lipscomb and Gino Marchetti to manhandle the other fellows when they had the pigskin. Then one day, as it is written, Shaw got hurt in a game, and YOU-ni-tass came in, hunched of shoulder, trotting kind of funny. He looked *crooked*, is how I always thought of him. Jagged. Sort of a gridiron Abraham Lincoln.

And on the first play the rookie threw a pass that went for a long touchdown. Only it was an interception; the touchdown went the other way.

For those of us in Baltimore, this seemed like the cruelest fate (however likely). Finally Baltimore was going to amount to something, and then, wouldn't you know it, Shaw gets taken from us. It seemed so terribly unfair, if perhaps exactly what we could expect for our workingman's town, where the swells passed through, without stopping, on their way to Washington or New York.

But then, there couldn't have been a mother's son anywhere who knew exactly what Unitas had in store for us. Marchetti, apparently, was the first one to understand. It was a couple of weeks later, and he was lying on the training table when the equipment manager, Fred Schubach, wondered out loud when Shaw might come back. Marchetti raised up a bit and said, "It doesn't matter. Unitas is the quarterback now."

Evidently all the other Colts nodded; they'd just been waiting for someone to dare express what they were beginning to sense. Marchetti had fought in the Battle of the Bulge when he was a teenager and thus, apparently, had developed a keen appreciation for things larger than life.

Of course, no matter whom John Constantine Unitas had played football for, it would've been Katie-bar-the-door. But perhaps greatness has never found such a fitting address. It wasn't only that Baltimore had such an inferiority complex, an awareness that all that the stuck-up outlanders knew of our fair city was that we had crabs and white marble steps in profusion and a dandy red-light district, the Block. Since H.L. Mencken (he who had declared, "I hate all sports as rabidly as a person who likes sports hates common sense") had died, the most famous Baltimorean was a stripper, Blaze Starr. The city hadn't had a winner since the Old Orioles of a century past. For that matter, until very recently Baltimore hadn't even *had* a major league team in the 1900s. Before the Colts arrived in 1947, the best athlete in town was a woman duckpin bowler named Toots Barger. Football? The biggest games in Baltimore had been when Johns Hopkins took on Susquehanna or Franklin & Marshall at homecoming.

But no mother ever took her children to her breast as old Bawlmer, Merlin (as we pronounced it), embraced the Colts. It wasn't just that they played on Sundays and thus finally made us "big league" in the eyes of the rest of a republic that was rapidly becoming coaxial-cabled together. No, the Colts were just folks, all around town, at crab feasts and bull roasts and what-have-you. Why, I knew I could go a few blocks to Moses' Sunoco station on York Road and see a bunch of Colts there, hanging out, kicking tires. If I'd had a good enough fake I.D., I could've even gotten into Sweeney's, up Greenmount Avenue and drunk beer with them. The Colts were real people, so we loved them even more as they went on their merry way to becoming champions of the world.

With each passing game, though, Unitas elevated above the others until, on Dec. 28, 1958, he entered the pantheon of gods. 'Twas then, of course, in Yankee Stadium itself, that he led us from behind to an overtime victory over the despised New Yorkers in the Greatest Game Ever Played. Yet even as we deified him, we still had it on the best authority that he remained one of the boys. Just because he was quarterback, he wasn't some glamour-puss.

Certainly he didn't look the part of a hero. This is how his teammate Alex Hawkins described Unitas when Hawkins first saw him in the locker room: "Here was a total mystery. [Unitas] was from Pennsylvania, but he looked so much like a Mississippi farmhand that I looked around for a mule. He had stooped shoulders, a chicken breast, thin bowed legs and long, dangling arms with crooked, mangled fingers."

Unitas didn't even have a quarterback's name. All by himself he redrew the profile of the quarterback. Always, before, it had been men of Old Stock who qualified to lead the pros. Baugh and Albert and Van Brocklin and Layne and Graham. (All right, Luckman was a Jew, but he was schooled in the WASP-y Ivy League.) Unitas was some hardscrabble Lithuanian, so what he did made a difference, because even if we'd never met a Lithuanian before, we knew that he was as smart a sonuvabitch as he was tough. Dammit, he was *our* Lithuanian.

They didn't have coaches with headphones and Polaroids and fax machines then, sitting on high, telling quarterbacks what plays to call. In those halcyon days, quarterbacks were field generals, not field lieutenants. And there was Unitas after he called a play (and probably checked off and called another play when he saw what the ruffians across the line were up to), shuffling back into the pocket, unfazed by the violent turbulence all around him, standing there in his hightops, waiting, looking, poised. I never saw war, so that is still my vision of manhood: Unitas stand-

ing courageously in the pocket, his left arm flung out in a diagonal to the upper deck, his right cocked for the business of passing, down amidst the mortals. Lock and load.

There, to Berry at the sideline. Or Moore. Or Jimmy Orr real long. Lenny Lyles. John Mackey. Hawkins. Ameche out of the backfield. My boyhood memory tells me Johnny U never threw an incompletion, let alone an interception, after that single debut mistake. Spoilsports who keep the numbers dispute that recollection, but they also assure me that he threw touchdown passes in 47 straight games. That figure has been threatened less seriously than even DiMaggio's sacred 56. Yes, I know there've been wonderful quarterbacks since Unitas hung up his hightops. I admit I'm prejudiced. But the best quarterback ever? The best player? Let me put it this way: If there were one game scheduled, Earth versus the Klingons, with the fate of the universe on the line, any person with his wits about him would have Johnny U calling the signals in the huddle, up under the center, back in the pocket.

I'VE ALWAYS WONDERED HOW people in olden times connected back to their childhoods. After all, we have hooks with the past. When most of us from the 20th century reminisce about growing up, we right away remember the songs and the athletes of any particular moment. Right?

A few years ago I saw Danny and the Juniors performing at a club, and all anybody wanted them to sing was *At the Hop*, which was their No. 1 smash back in 1958, the year Unitas led the Colts to that first, fabled championship. About a year after I saw Danny, I read that he had committed suicide. I always assumed it was because no matter how many years had passed, nobody would let him escape from singing *At the Hop*, exactly as he did in 1958.

Unlike songs, athletes, inconveniently, get on. They grow old. Johnny U couldn't keep on throwing passes. He aged. He even let his crew cut grow out. Luckily for me, after I grew up (as it were) and became a sportswriter, I never covered him. Oh, I went to his restaurant, and I saw him on TV, and I surely never forgot him. Whenever Walter Iooss, the photographer, and I would get together, we would talk about Johnny U the way most men talk about caressing beautiful women. But I never had anything to do with Unitas professionally. That was good. I could keep my boy's memories unsullied.

Then, about five years ago, I finally met him at a party. When we were introduced he said, "It's nice to meet you, Mr. Deford." That threw me into a tailspin. *No, no, no. Don't you understand? I'm not Mr. Deford. You're Mr. Unitas. You're Johnny U. You're my boyhood idol. I can't ever be Mr. Deford with you, because you have to always be number 19, so I can always be a kid.* But I didn't explain that to him. I was afraid he would think I was too sappy. I just said, "It's nice to meet you, too, Mr. Unitas," and shook his crippled hand.

A couple of years later I went down to Baltimore and gave a speech for a charity. What they gave me as a thank-you present was a football, autographed by Himself. When you're not a child anymore and you write about athletes, you tend to take 'em as run-of-the-mill human beings. Anyway, I do. I have only one other athlete's autograph, from Bill Russell, who, along with Unitas, is the other great star of the '50s who changed his sport all by himself.

After I got that autographed Unitas football, every now and then I'd pick it up and fondle it. I still do, too, even though Johnny Unitas is dead now, and I can't be a boy anymore. Ultimately, you see, what he conveyed to his teammates and to Baltimore and to a wider world was the utter faith that he could do it. He could make it work. Somehow, he could win. He *would* win. It almost didn't matter when he actually couldn't. The point was that with Johnny U, it always seemed possible. You so very seldom get that, even with the best of them. Johnny U's talents were his own. The belief he gave us was his gift. . . .

UNITAS STOOD tall in a 45–17 win over the Redskins in 1964, one of the three seasons in which he was the NFL's player of the year.

1996 | COWBOYS CORNERBACK Deion Sanders was also an offensive threat against the Steelers in Super Bowl XXX | *Photograph by* RICHARD MACKSON

1962 | THE COLTS' Jimmy Orr beat tight coverage for a touchdown catch against the 49ers | *Photograph by* WALTER IOOSS JR.

> **Artifacts**

Bling of Truth

Super Bowl rings don't lie: The only people entitled to wear them are NFL champions

SUPER BOWL I

Packers 35, Chiefs 10

SUPER BOWL III

Jets 16, Colts 7

SUPER BOWL IV

Chiefs 23, Vikings 7

SUPER BOWL V

Colts 16, Cowboys 13

SUPER BOWL VI

Cowboys 24, Dolphins 3

SUPER BOWL VIII

Dolphins 24, Vikings 7

SUPER BOWL X

Steelers 21, Cowboys 17

SUPER BOWL XVIII

Raiders 38, Redskins 9

SUPER BOWL XXI

Giants 39, Broncos 20

SUPER BOWL XXIV

49ers 55, Broncos 10

SUPER BOWL XXVI

Redskins 37, Bills 24

SUPER BOWL XXXIII

Broncos 34, Falcons 19

SUPER BOWL XXXIV

Rams 23, Titans 16

SUPER BOWL XXXVI

Patriots 20, Rams 17

FORTY NINERS WINNERS

1976 | STEELERS TACKLE Ernie Holmes shed a blocker as he pressured Roger Staubach in Super Bowl X | *Photograph by* JOHN BIEVER

1972 | PACKERS TACKLE Mike McCoy had mayhem in mind but couldn't reach 49ers QB Steve Spurrier before he let fly | *Photograph by* JOHN BIEVER

from THE TOUGHEST JOB IN SPORTS | BY PETER KING

SI August 17,1998

I N 1948 CHICAGO BEARS COACH

George Halas traded disappointing rookie Bobby Layne, who eventually became one of the NFL's top quarterbacks with the Detroit Lions. In the late '50s the Pittsburgh Steelers gave up on young signal-callers John Unitas and Jack Kemp, and kept, among others, Vic Eaton and Jack Scarbath. Warren Moon wasn't among the 334 players selected in the '78 draft. The following year Joe Montana was a third-round pick. In '83 the Lions felt so good about incumbent Eric Hipple that they passed on Jim Kelly and Dan Marino. In '91 at least 10 teams had Browning Nagle rated higher than Brett Favre.

Of the 10 quarterbacks selected among the top 10 picks in the regular or supplemental draft during the 1990s, only the New England Patriots' Drew Bledsoe has performed at a Pro Bowl–caliber level. Seven have struggled mightily (Dave Brown, Rick Mirer, Heath Shuler, Trent Dilfer, Kerry Collins) or been abject failures (Andre Ware, David Klingler).

Twelve of the 30 projected starting quarterbacks this fall were selected in the third round or later, and two more were undrafted. The quest for a quarterback who may one day lead a team to a Super Bowl is getting more and more like the lottery: Take your best shot, then cross your fingers.

Why is it so hard to unearth a good quarterback? Let's start with this premise: Quarterback is the most complex position in sports. A pitcher has to be precise in his pitch location and outwit the hitter; a point guard must direct his teammates and adjust on the fly to make a play work; a hockey goalie must be athletic and fearless. A quarterback has to be able to do and be all of those things. "I'd say quarterback's the toughest position," says Phoenix Suns coach Danny Ainge, a former all-state high school quarterback, major league shortstop and All-Star NBA guard. "A quarterback has to be a leader, have good vision, be physically and mentally tough and be athletic. He has to be able to read defenses and figure out what the other team's giving him."

"Every fall Sunday, you're the nerve center for a city, a county, a state, a region," says Boomer Esiason, who played quarterback for 14 NFL seasons. "You step behind center, and millions of people watch to see what you'll do next. The pressure kills some guys. There's no other job like it in sports." . . .

1942 | REDSKINS QUARTERBACK Sammy Baugh held most of the NFL's passing records when he retired in 1952. *Photograph by* AP

> ### > SI's TOP 25

The Quarterbacks

JOHN ELWAY
Photograph by TIM DEFRISCO

FRAN TARKENTON
Photograph by NEIL LEIFER

BOBBY LAYNE
Photograph by NFL

TERRY BRADSHAW
Photograph by NEIL LEIFER

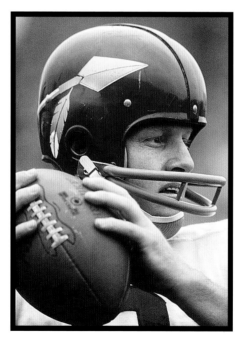

SONNY JURGENSEN
Photograph by FRED ROE

BRETT FAVRE
Photograph by DARREN HAUCK

JOE MONTANA

Photograph by ANDY HAYT

TROY AIKMAN

Photograph by ROB TRINGALI

FRITZ POLLARD

Photograph by BROWN UNIVERSITY ARCHIVES

DAN MARINO

Photograph by BOB ROSATO

TROY AIKMAN

SAMMY BAUGH

TERRY BRADSHAW

TOM BRADY

LEN DAWSON

JOHN ELWAY

BRETT FAVRE

DAN FOUTS

BENNY FRIEDMAN

OTTO GRAHAM

BOB GRIESE

SONNY JURGENSEN

JIM KELLY

BOBBY LAYNE

SID LUCKMAN

PEYTON MANNING

DAN MARINO

JOE MONTANA

JOE NAMATH

FRITZ POLLARD

BART STARR

ROGER STAUBACH

FRAN TARKENTON

JOHNNY UNITAS

STEVE YOUNG

1962 | THE TOE, Lou Groza, was a Hall of Fame tackle for the Browns for 12 years, and their stalwart kicker for 21 | *Photograph by* TONY TOMSIC

THE ULTIMATE WINNER

BY PAUL ZIMMERMAN

Heading an offense tailored to his unique skills, San Francisco's Joe Montana enjoyed unparalleled success as a quarterback, including victories in four Super Bowls. —*from* SI, AUGUST 13, 1990

WHEN SAN FRANcisco 49ers coach Bill Walsh talks about offensive football, he eventually mentions the "quick, slashing strokes" of attack. He'll use analogies with tennis and boxing, even warfare, which was why he was so taken with quarterback Joe Montana's nimble feet. A quick, slashing attack needs a quick-footed quarterback. The statuesque quarterback who can throw the ball 60 yards downfield has never been Walsh's type. And when he refined his offense to blend with Montana's skills, Walsh introduced the X factor, which was the great escape talent of his quarterback—elusiveness, body control, the ability to throw while in the grasp of an opponent.

"A lot of our offense was play-action," Walsh says, "and I learned through my experience that on a play-pass you have to expect an unblocked man just when you're trying to throw the ball. If you can throw and take the hit—TD. If you can avoid him, so much the better. We were on the cutting edge of Joe's ability. He was gifted at avoiding and throwing. We practiced the scrambling, off-balance throw. It was a carefully practiced thing"

Finally it all came into focus in the '81 postseason, in one momentous play, the last-minute touchdown pass to wideout Dwight Clark that buried the Dallas Cowboys in the NFC Championship Game. The play will always be known as The Catch—Montana scrambling to his right, with three Cowboys clutching at him; the off-balance throw; and finally Clark, on a breakoff route, ducking inside, then cutting back—just the way he and Joe had practiced on their own so many times in camp.

The Super Bowl was an anticlimax. The 49ers beat the Bengals 26–21, with Montana taking MVP honors. In each of the 49ers' next two Super Bowls, he again was matched with a consensus All-Pro, Dan Marino of the Miami Dolphins in '85 and Boomer Esiason of Cincinnati in '89. Montana had gone in as the second-best quarterback each time and won. By the time of the 49ers' fourth Super Bowl, in '90, everyone had learned, and the question was only how badly would Montana and the 49ers beat John Elway and the Denver Broncos?

The first talk of Montana being the greatest of all came in Bay Area circles after the '82 Super Bowl, as put forth by a couple of old 49ers quarterbacks. John Brodie said it, flat out, and people laughed. Frankie Albert said, "At 25, he's ahead of Unitas, Van Brocklin, Waterfield . . . all the immortals."

Based on the NFL quarterback rating system, Montana's '89 season was the best anyone has ever had—the highest rating (112.4) and third-highest completion percentage (70.2) in history. But those are just numbers. The 49ers swept through the playoffs and the Super Bowl like a broom, trouncing Denver 55–10 to repeat as NFL champions. Their efficiency was frightening, and Montana was the master.

If you want to highlight one game during the season, try the game in Philadelphia on Sept. 24. Some people call it the finest Montana has ever played. For three quarters the 49ers' offense was falling apart. Montana had been sacked seven times, with one more to come. He had tripped twice while setting up and had fallen in the end zone for a safety. The Eagles were coming at him like crazy, and the 49ers were down 21–10 with 10 seconds gone in the fourth quarter. Then Montana threw four touchdown passes into the teeth of the Eagles' rush to pull out a 38–28 victory. His fourth-quarter stats read 11 completions in 12 attempts for 227 yards, and he scrambled for 19 more.

"Worried? Oh, hell, yes, we were worried," 49ers tackle Harris Barton says of the Eagles' assault on Montana. "Joe gets that glazed look in his eyes, and you know he's been shellacked. It wasn't a good situation to be in. We'd get to the sideline and Joe would say, 'O.K., let's get this thing settled down.' I was just amazed that he could line up at all after getting smacked in the head by Reggie White."

If you want to make a case for Montana as the greatest quarterback who ever played the game, there it is. Toughness. The great ones all had it—Unitas, Graham, Baugh, Waterfield, Tittle, Bradshaw. When you add Montana's finesse, the sensuous and fluid qualities that Walsh saw at the beginning, plus his uncanny accuracy—no one has ever thrown the short crossing pattern with a better touch—you've got a special package. . . .

JOE COOL was an apt nickname for Montana, who engineered 31 fourth-quarter come-from-behind wins.

1974 | FIVE-TIME Pro Bowler Len Hauss anchored the center of the Redskins' offensive line | *Photograph by* NEIL LEIFER

2003 | THE RAIDERS' Barret Robbins had his own signals to call before he snapped the ball to Rich Gannon | *Photograph by* RON SCHWANE

2001 | VIKINGS WIDEOUT Randy Moss took matters into his own hand to make this reception against the Steelers | *Photograph by* DAMIAN STROHMEYER

1983 | THE CHARGERS' Mike Williams got up high to cover Dolphins tight end Bruce Hardy, who went even higher for this catch | *Photograph by* WALTER IOOSS JR.

> Artifacts

Tickets to Paradise

The price has gone up over the years, but a ducat still gets you through the turnstile and then makes a perfect souvenir

JETS VS. RAIDERS *August 23, 1963*

BEARS VS. ALL-STARS *September 23, 1938*

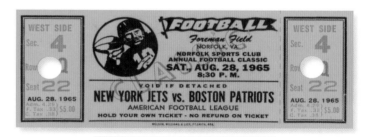

JETS VS. PATRIOTS *August 28, 1965*

VIKINGS VS. EAGLES *August 12, 1967*

BEARS VS. CARDINALS *December 1, 1946*

DODGERS VS. EAGLES *November 7, 1937*

BEARS VS. COLLEGE ALL STARS *August 28, 1942*

CARDINALS VS. LIONS *August 15, 1959*

BROWNS VS. COLLEGE ALL-STARS *August 6, 1965*

1962 | THE 49ERS didn't measure up to the Browns in a 13–10 Cleveland victory in San Francisco in December | *Photograph by* NEIL LEIFER

1973 | VIKINGS QB Fran Tarkenton knew exactly what he needed to get past the Cowboys in the NFC title game | *Photograph by* NEIL LEIFER

ZERO OF THE LIONS

BY GEORGE PLIMPTON

For a professional amateur given a chance to play quarterback for Detroit, there were many things to worry about, but none more daunting than the pit. —*from* SI, SEPTEMBER 7, 1964

ONE OF THE TROUBLES with wearing a football helmet was that it closed off the outside world, the noise of the crowd, the cheering as the contests wore on—all of this just a murmur—leaving my mind to work away busily inside the amphitheater of the helmet. Voices, my own, spoke quite clearly, offering consolation, encouragement and paternal advice of a particularly galling sort: "The thing to be is calm, son, and remember not to snatch back from the ball until you get it set in your palm."

"I'll hang on to the ball," I murmured back.

"But"—the portentous voice came again like the Ghost's in *Hamlet*—"you must not dally, son. On the handoffs you must get the ball to the halfbacks with dispatch."

These pronouncements were accompanied by short, visual vignettes, subliminal, but which seemed to flash inside my helmet with the clarity of a television screen in a dark room—tumultuous scenes of big tackles and guards in what seemed a landslide, a cliff of them toppling toward me like a slow-moving object in a dream, as I lay in some sort of a depression gaping up in resigned dismay. Raymond Berry, the knowledgeable Baltimore receiver, once told me that I would survive a scrimmage if I played his position and was sure to stay out of what he referred to as the "pit"—a designation that often came to mind just before my participation in scrimmages. It was an area, as he described it, along the line of scrimmage, perhaps 10 yards deep, where at the centering of the ball the Neanderthal struggle began between the opposing linemen. The struggle raged within a relatively restricted area that was possible to avoid. Berry had wandered into the pit only three times—coming back to catch poorly-thrown passes—and he spoke of each instance as one might speak of a serious automobile accident. The particulars were embalmed in his memory in absolute clarity: that year, in that city, at such-and-such a game, during such-and-such a quarter, when so-and-so, the quarterback, threw the ball short, his arm jogged by a red-dogging linebacker, so that Berry had to run back toward the scrimmage line so many yards to catch it, and it was so-and-so, the 290-pounder, who reached an arm out of the ruck of the pit and dragged him down into it.

"One thing to remember when you do get hit," Berry told me in his soft Texas accent, "is to try to fall in the foetus position. Curl up around the ball, and keep your limbs from being extended, because there'll be other people coming up out of the pit to see you don't move any, and one of them landing on an arm that's outstretched, y'know, can snap it."

"Right," I said.

"But the big thing is just stay out of that area."

"Sure," I said.

But when I arrived to train with the Lions I disregarded his advice. What I had to try to play was quarterback, because the essence of the game was involved with that position. The coaches agreed, if reluctantly, and after the front office had made me sign some papers absolving them of any responsibility, I became the "last-string" quarterback, and thus stood in Berry's pit each time I walked up behind the center to call signals. He was right, of course. One of my first plays landed me in the pit. It was a simple handoff. Opposite me the linebackers were all close up, shouting, "Jumbo! Jumbo! Jumbo!" which is one of the Lion code cries to rush the quarterback. When the snap came I fumbled the ball, gaping at it, mouth ajar, as it rocked back and forth gaily at my feet, and I flung myself on it, my subconscious shrilling, "Foetus! Foetus!" as I tried to draw myself in like a frightened pill bug, and I heard the sharp strange whack of gear, the grunts—and then a sudden weight whooshed the air out of me.

It was Dave Lloyd, a 250-pound linebacker, who got to me. A whistle blew and I clambered up, seeing him grin inside his helmet, to discover that the quick sense of surprise that I had survived was replaced by a pulsation of fury that I had not done better. I swore lustily at my clumsiness, hopping mad, near to throwing the ball into the ground, and eager to form a huddle to call another play and try again. The players were all standing up, some with their helmets off, many with big grins, and I heard someone calling, "Hey, man, hey, man!" and someone else called out, "Beautiful, real beautiful." I sensed then that an initiation had been performed, a blooding ceremony. Linebacker Wayne Walker said, "Welcome to pro ball." Something in the tone of it made it not only in reference to the quick horror of what had happened when I fumbled but in appreciation that I had gone through something that made me, if tenuously, one of them, and they stood for a while on the field watching me savor it. . . .

THE PAPER LION was a big zero on the Detroit bench between Nick Pietrosante (left) and Jim Gibbons.

1995 | CHIEFS BACK Marcus Allen scored the 100th of his 123 career rushing TDs, in Denver | *Photograph by* TIM DEFRISCO

T AKE A KNEE, BILL BELICHICK thought. Play it safe, kill the clock and don't put your young quarterback in a position to blow the Super Bowl. This was one option that Belichick, the cerebral coach of the New England Patriots, considered on Sunday night as the Louisiana Superdome shook with energy and the roof seemed ready to cave in on his team.

Then, with 81 seconds left and the Patriots locked in a 17–17 tie with the resurgent St. Louis Rams, Belichick's head deferred to his heart. Although his tired team had squandered a 14-point, fourth-quarter lead, Belichick decided that kneeling was for wimps. Instead his underdog Patriots and their undaunted 24-year-old quarterback, Tom Brady, would deliver one of the most thrilling finishes the sport has known.

As New England prepared to take over at its 17-yard line with no timeouts, Belichick conferred with his offensive coordinator, Charlie Weis, who agreed that an aggressive approach was the right one. "O.K., let's go for it," Belichick said. When Weis relayed the decision to Brady, he could see the surprise in the second-year passer's eyes. There was no fear, however. "With a quarterback like Brady, going for the win is not that dangerous," Belichick explained later, "because he's not going to make a mistake."

What Brady did as those seconds ticked off sent chills through the spines of fans from Cape Cod to Kandahar. Aside from a pair of clock-killing spikes, he completed five of six passes for 53 yards to set up Adam Vinatieri's 48-yard field goal, which sailed through the uprights for a 20–17 victory as time expired. Brady, whose statistics had been unimpressive until that final drive, was voted the MVP of what will go down as one of the greatest Super Bowls.

For patriots and Patriots, this Sunday was as super as it gets: One hundred forty-five days after the Sept. 11 terrorist attacks that stunned a country and stalled an NFL season, the ultimate game provided the ultimate diversion. In beating the vaunted Rams, who were two-touchdown favorites, New England completed an amazing journey no reasonable forecaster could have predicted. With chants of *U-S-A!* filling the stadium, the Pats staged a clinic on the nation's bedrock values—teamwork, bucking the odds, overcoming adversity and refusing to wilt in the face of danger. . . .

2002 | VINDICATING BELICHICK'S gamble, Vinatieri (4) thumped home the game-winner as the clock ran out, giving New England an improbable title. | *Photograph by* JOHN W. MCDONOUGH

2005 | BROWNS DB Gary Baxter got his hand on a pass before Green Bay's Terrence Murphy (85) or Antonio Chatman could | *Photograph by* JOHN H. REID III

1961 | LIONS LINEBACKER Joe Schmidt made sure the Packers' Jim Taylor had no place to go but down | *Photograph by* MARVIN E. NEWMAN

2006 | A BURST of speed couldn't free Jets wideout Laveranues Coles from the Patriots' Eugene Wilson (26) and Ellis Hobbs | *Photograph by* MIKE EHRMANN

2006 | THE JAGUARS' Ernest Wilford tried in vain to overcome coverage by the Eagles' Sheldon Brown (24) | *Photograph by* DAVID BERGMAN

> SI's **TOP 25** *The Offensive Linemen*

DAN DIERDORF
Photograph by NEIL LEIFER

JIM OTTO
Photograph by JAMES FLORES

MEL HEIN
Photograph by AP

JIM RINGO
Photograph by LEFEBVRE-LUEBKE

ANTHONY MUNOZ
Photograph by PETER BROUILLET

GENE UPSHAW
Photograph by HEINZ KLUETMEIER

JIM PARKER
Photograph by DARRYL NORENBERG

CLYDE (BULLDOG) TURNER
Photograph by NFL

MIKE WEBSTER
Photograph by TSN

ROOSEVELT BROWN
Photograph by DAN RUBIN

BOB BROWN

ROOSEVELT BROWN

LOU CREEKMUR

JOE DeLAMIELLEURE

DAN DIERDORF

FRANK GATSKI

FORREST GREGG

RUSS GRIMM

JOHN HANNAH

MEL HEIN

JIM LANGER

LARRY LITTLE

MIKE MUNCHAK

ANTHONY MUNOZ

JONATHAN OGDEN

JIM OTTO

JIM PARKER

JIM RINGO

BOB ST. CLAIR

BILLY SHAW

JACKIE SLATER

DWIGHT STEPHENSON

CLYDE (BULLDOG) TURNER

GENE UPSHAW

MIKE WEBSTER

1948 | BEARS QBS (from left) Bobby Layne, Johnny Lujack and Sid Luckman took target practice | *Photograph by* HANK WALKER

1979 | GEORGIA ROSENBLOOM put her best foot forward as the Rams' owner | *Photograph by* RICHARD MACKSON

'I'LL DO ANYTHING
I CAN GET AWAY WITH'

BY DAPHNE HURFORD

What's a little holding and biting among NFL linemen? For Conrad Dobler, "anything goes" on a football field seemed to mean everything short of a neutron bomb. — *from* SI, JULY 25, 1977

ONE OF THE QUESTIONS on the NFL's personnel survey form is, "Did you take up football for any particular reason?" Conrad Dobler's answer was, "It is still the only sport where there is controlled violence mixed with careful technical planning. Football is still a very physical game."

What Dobler, the All-Pro right guard for the St. Louis Cardinals, means by "controlled violence," "careful technical planning" and "a very physical game" is that "I'll do anything I can get away with to protect my quarterback." And according to his opponents, what Dobler gets away with is holding, eye gouging, face-mask twisting, leg-whipping, tripping, even biting.

Outside St. Louis, Dobler is considered the dirtiest player in the league. In one game Dobler's tactics so infuriated Merlin Olsen, the now-retired defensive tackle of the Los Angeles Rams, that Olsen swore he would never utter Dobler's name again. However, there is one player who has good reason to utter Dobler's name in his prayers—Cardinal quarterback Jim Hart. Thanks to the protection—legal or otherwise—afforded by Dobler and his linemates, Hart has been sacked only 41 times over the last three seasons, an NFL low. Among others who recognize Dobler's prowess are the NFL coaches, who have twice picked him to start in the Pro Bowl.

Dobler was just another obscure lineman until 1974, his third season in the league, when some Minnesota Vikings jokingly requested rabies shots before a game against the Cardinals. Suddenly Dobler had acquired an image. "What you need when you play against Dobler," said one rival, "is a string of garlic buds around your neck and a wooden stake. If they played every game under a full moon, Dobler would make All Pro. He must be the only guy in the league who sleeps in a casket."

Dobler says that he holds no more than any other player, that he would get caught more often if he did, and that reports of his dastardly deeds have been exaggerated. In the next breath he says that rules are made to be broken and adds, with a slightly superior air, "If you're going to break the rules, you've got to have a little style and class." Asked if he really bites opponents, Dobler usually replies that he would never do such a tasteless thing, believing as he does in good oral hygiene. Of course, he adds, "If someone stuck his hand in your face mask and put his fingers in your mouth, what would you do?"

While Dobler insists that he is an aggrieved party as far as holding is concerned, he willingly offers a few hints on the best way to hold a defensive lineman or a blitzing linebacker. "Always keep your hands inside your chest because it's much harder for the referees to see them when they're in there," he says, "and if a guy does get past you, grab his face mask, not his jersey." Dobler also recommends "hooking"—clamping the opponent with your arm and dragging him down—as an effective means of detaining defenders.

"Sometimes I hold by accident," he says. "I get my hand caught in a face mask. But always remember this: At no time do my fingers leave my hand."

Surprisingly, Dobler rarely uses his tongue on rivals. "You have to get just the right comment to make them mad," he says. "Verbal abuse could take all day. A faster and more efficient way to aggravate and intimidate people is to knock the stuffing out of them." Dobler particularly likes to aggravate and intimidate Pro Bowlers, first-round draft choices and players whose salaries are higher than his $50,000 a year. "Of course I'm vindictive," he says. "I was a fifth-round draft choice. . . ."

Drafted by the Cardinals in 1972, Dobler was released before his rookie season. Luckily for him a number of the Cardinals' linemen were injured early on, and they re-signed Dobler in time for their third game. "When I came back I decided that I'd just play my own game," he says. "I'd do what I do best and make the other guys play into my hands, make them have to beat me."

Jim Hanifan, St. Louis' offensive line coach, says of his right guard, "You'd have to kill him to beat him." Dobler smiles. "When you're fighting in the dirt for a position, climbing up from the bottom, you know what it is to compete," he says. "If we both wanted it, I'd want it more. I'd mow 'em right down with no compassion, no mercy." . . .

DURING HIS 10 years in the NFL trenches Dobler, though often called the league's dirtiest player, earned three trips to the Pro Bowl.

2007 | BAREHEADED BEAR Darwin Walker (99) faced down the Giants at Chicago's goal line during a 21–16 loss to New York | *Photograph by* JOHN BIEVER

2008 | THE REF got a good look at the airborne assault of Chiefs running back Larry Johnson when he met resistance from the Broncos | *Photograph by* JOHN BIEVER

A VIKING CONQUEST

BY STEVE RUSHIN

Alan Page, the first defensive player to be named the NFL's MVP, was a fearsome presence on the field . . . and in the lobby of a Holiday Inn if you were a young fan looking for an autograph.
—*from SI, JULY 31, 2000*

YOU COULDN'T BUY A number 88 Vikings jersey in Minnesota in 1974. You could buy the 10 of Fran Tarkenton or the 44 of Chuck Foreman, but if you wanted the 88 of Alan Page your parents had to find a blank purple football shirt and have the numbers ironed on. As far as I know, my parents were the only ones who ever did. The jersey became my security blanket—what psychologists call a "transition object," the item that sustains a child in moments away from his mother. I wore the shirt until it disintegrated in the wash and blew away one day like dandelion spores.

I grew up in the town in which the Vikings played their home games, in the decade in which they played in four Super Bowls. Yet even in Bloomington, Minn., in the 1970s, I was alone among my schoolmates in worshipping Page, who was fearsome and had a reputation for brooding silence, a reputation that I scarcely knew of as an eight-year-old. I knew only that Page had gone to Notre Dame, that he was genuinely great—the first defensive player to be named MVP of the NFL—and that his Afro sometimes resembled Mickey Mouse ears when he removed his helmet. Lithe and almost feline, Page went wherever the ballcarrier was, often pulling the runner down with one hand. He won his MVP award in his fifth year. I at once loved Alan Page and knew nothing whatsoever about him.

Then one unfathomable day in September '74, the month in which I turned eight, a second-grade classmate named Troy Chaika invited me to a Saturday night sleepover at the Airport Holiday Inn, which his father managed and where the Vikings, as everyone knew, bivouacked on the night before each home game. I could meet the players when they checked in and, if I asked politely and addressed each of them as "Mister," get their autographs, a prospect that thrilled and terrified me in equal measure. So every night for two weeks, toothbrush in hand, I practiced my pitch to the bathroom mirror: "Please, Mr. Page, may I have your autograph?"

Time crawled, clocks ticked backward, but, after an eternity, Saturday came. My mom—God bless her, for it must have pained her beyond words—allowed me to leave the house in my 88 jersey, now literally in tatters, the kind of shirt worn by men in comic strips who have been marooned on a tiny desert island with one palm tree.

So I took my place in the Holiday Inn lobby—Bic pen in one damp hand, spiral notebook in the other—and recited my mantra rapid-fire to myself, like Hail Marys on a rosary: "*Please Mr.PagemayIhaveyour autograph?PleaseMr.PagemayIhaveyourautograph?PleaseMr.Page. . . .*"

Moments before the Vikings' 8 p.m. arrival, my friend's father, the innkeeper, cheerily reminded me to be polite and that the players would in turn oblige me. "Except Page," he added offhandedly, in the oblivious way of adults. "Don't ask him. He doesn't sign autographs."

Which is how I came to be blinking back tears when the Vikings walked into the Holiday Inn, wearing Stetsons and suede pants and sideburns like shag-carpet samples. Their shirt collars flapped like pterodactyl wings. They were truly terrifying men, none more so than Page, whose entrance—alone, an overnight bag slung over his shoulder—cleaved a group of bellhops and veteran teenage autograph hounds, who apparently knew to give the man a wide berth.

Page strode purposefully toward the stairwell. I choked as he breezed past; I was unable to speak, a small and insignificant speck whose cheeks, armpits and tear ducts were suddenly bursting into flames. It was to be an early lesson in life's manifold disappointments: two weeks of excruciating anticipation dashed in as many seconds. Still, I had never seen Page outside a television set and couldn't quite believe he was incarnate, so—my chicken chest heaving, hyperventilation setting in—I continued to watch as he paused at the stairs, turned and looked back at the lobby, evidently having forgotten to pick up his room key.

But he hadn't forgotten any such thing. No, Page walked directly toward me, took the Bic from my trembling hand and signed his name, *ALAN PAGE*, in one grand flourish. He smiled and put his hand on top of my head, as if palming a grapefruit. Then he disappeared into the stairwell, leaving me to stand there in the lobby, slack-jawed, forming a small puddle of admiration and urine. . . .

QUICK AND STRONG, Page was the first defensive player to be named the league's MVP, in 1971.

2008 | THE UPSIDE of this collision with Atlanta's Erik Coleman (above, left) was a TD for Green Bay's Donald Driver | *Photograph by* HEINZ KLUETMEIER

2007 | THE REDSKINS' Clinton Portis wasn't grandstanding when he ended up standing on his head in the end zone against the Giants | *Photograph by* NICK WASS

1991 | NEW ORLEANS tackle Stan Brock was sitting pretty during a Saints victory over the Falcons in Atlanta | *Photograph by* JOHN BIEVER

2003 | BILLS DEFENSIVE tackle Sam Adams scored a rare touchdown after intercepting a Tom Brady pass | *Photograph by* DAMIAN STROHMEYER

AN IRON MAN AND EVERYMAN

BY ALAN SHIPNUCK

At 38, Brett Favre was enjoying one of his finest NFL seasons. But his greatest attribute was the devotion he inspired in those he touched. —*from* SI, DECEMBER 10, 2007

THERE IS NO HAPPIER PLACE than Green Bay on a Sunday evening after the Packers have won. The beer tastes better, the girls are even prettier, and few seem to notice the bite in the air. In a town defined by its team, civic temperament can be quantified on a scoreboard. The epicenter of this game-day good cheer a few weeks ago, in the moments after the Packers had defeated Carolina, was adjacent to Lambeau Field, just across Holmgren Way, a block over from Lombardi Avenue: Brett Favre's Steakhouse, located at 1004 Brett Favre Pass. The restaurant is a 20,000-square-foot temple to the Packers' quarterback, and in this loud, lively gathering only one person was missing—the man for whom the restaurant and the street are named.

In his 16th winter in Green Bay, Favre has turned into Gatsby, throwing a party he no longer enjoys. While his family and friends were reliving every detail of his three-touchdown performance against Carolina, Favre was at home a couple of miles away, stretched out on his couch, watching that day's NFL highlights and cuddling with his lapdog, Charlie. "As I've gotten older, I've become more of a loner," Favre says. "You've just been out there in front of 80,000 screaming people, everyone watching every move you make, the pressure of all that—it's fine and dandy for three hours, but afterward. . . ."

If Favre is weary, it's only because he has given so much of himself to Green Bay through the years. "He means everything to these people," says Donald Driver, who's in his ninth season catching Favre's passes. "He's not only our leader—he's the symbol of the franchise, of the whole town."

When Favre decided to return for the 2007 season, even die-hard Cheeseheads must have been hoping only that he would not tarnish his legacy. What no one expected was that Favre would reinvent himself yet again, enjoying one of his best years at age 38 while cajoling a talented but callow team to a stunning 10–2 record. Along the way he passed two significant milestones for quarterbacks, overtaking Dan Marino atop the alltime list in touchdown passes and victories by a starter. But one record above all others speaks to what Favre is made of: his Ripkenesque streak of consecutive starts at quarterback, which stands at 249—more than five seasons ahead of the next player on the list, Peyton Manning. Through pills and booze, through cancer and car crashes and heart attacks, he has played on. Once reckless on and off the field, Favre has matured before our eyes while never losing his boyish love for the game. "I've always shown up, I've always been prepared, I practice every day," he says. "I practice hard. I study. No matter what happens on the field, I never point blame at anybody else. Everything I do comes back to leadership."

It is for his perseverance and his passion that SI honors Favre with the 54th Sportsman of the Year award. But there is more to his story than on-field heroics. On game day the whole of Green Bay may live and die on Favre's rocket right arm, but his greatest legacy lies in how many people he has touched between Sundays.

The intensity of Favre's relationship with the Packers faithful goes far beyond mere longevity. He arrived in Green Bay in 1992 through a trade with the Atlanta Falcons, and in the third game of the season came off the bench to lead a madcap comeback against the Cincinnati Bengals. He has refused to leave the starting lineup ever since, harnessing his hair-on-fire style to win an unprecedented three MVP awards (1995, '96, '97) and lead Green Bay to a Super Bowl triumph following the '96 season.

But the success was leavened by personal setbacks and heartache, among them Brett's addiction to the painkiller Vicodin, Deanna's bout with breast cancer and the death of Brett's father, Irvin, from a heart attack. During each crisis, the Favres were overwhelmed by the outpouring of support in Green Bay—bags of letters, innumerable prayer circles and many kind wishes murmured in the grocery aisle.

"People here treat us like family, and I think they care for us like family," says Deanna. "Because of everything we've been through, they don't see Brett as untouchable or as some kind of superhero. And they've been through it with us." . . .

A GOD in Green Bay, Favre was worshipped as much for his human struggles as for his superhuman heroics while he was the leader of the Pack.

2007 | NUTCRACKER DRILL: Patriots linebacker Tedy Bruschi applied the clamps to Redskins tight end Chris Cooley | *Photograph by* HEINZ KLUETMEIER

1976 | STEEL HURTIN': Pittsburgh's Jack Lambert (58) used a headlock to arrest the forward motion of Baltimore's Lydell Mitchell | *Photograph by* WALTER IOOSS JR.

I T WILL BE MANY YEARS BEFORE we see anything approaching the vision of hell that Chicago inflicted on the poor New England Patriots Sunday in Super Bowl XX. It was near perfect, an exquisite mesh of talent and system, defensive football carried to its highest degree. It was a great roaring wave that swept through the playoffs, gathering force and momentum, until it finally crashed home in pro football's showcase game.

The game wasn't exciting. So what? Go down to Bourbon Street if you want excitement. It wasn't competitive. The verdict on Chicago's 46–10 victory was in after two Patriot series. Don't feel cheated. Louis–Schmeling II wasn't very competitive, either. Nor was the British cavalry charge at Balaklava, but Tennyson wrote a poem about it. This game transcended the ordinary standards we use in judging football. It was historic.

The events of the next few weeks and months will determine if this is the beginning of a mighty defensive dynasty or its culmination. The forces of erosion already were at work. Buddy Ryan, the assistant coach who crafted this defense, was close to the Philadelphia head coaching job when his work was done in New Orleans. With two minutes to go, the defensive players gathered around Mike McCaskey, the Bears' president, and practically begged him to do everything he could to keep Ryan. "Dan Hampton was our spokesman," strong safety Dave Duerson said. "He told Mr. McCaskey that if we lose Buddy Ryan we'll be a good defensive unit, but if we keep him we'll be in the Super Bowl the next five years." Such is the hold that Ryan has on his players; his is a driving spirit that causes hard-eyed veterans like middle linebacker Mike Singletary to say, "Without him we don't have much. I feel honored to have been coached by him."

Money problems could inflict further damage. Right end Richard Dent, the Super Bowl MVP, is in a sticky salary situation. He could be gone, as Todd Bell and Al Harris were from last season's team. Others could follow. Win a title and the price of poker goes up.

O.K., let's not look for trouble. Mike Ditka's Bears have given Chicago its first title in any major professional sport since 1963, when Ditka himself played tight end for those champion Bears. And Ryan's defense, which virtually eliminates traditional positions, put together an astonishing string of conquests, a three-game playoff series that has never been duplicated. . . .

2005 | END-ZONE REFLECTIONS occupied Chargers runner LaDainian
Tomlinson at Philadelphia's Lincoln Financial Field | *Photograph by* SIMON BRUTY

2005 | A MONTH later, the goal line and Tomlinson were in focus as
LT vaulted for a TD against Buffalo | *Photograph by* PETER READ MILLER

1963 | WILLIE GALIMORE (28) and Mike Ditka (89) were keys to the Bears' offense on a championship team known for its D | *Photograph by* JAMES DRAKE

1954 | PAUL BROWN looked dapper even while squatting in the mud during the title game in which his Browns beat the Lions 56–10 | *Photograph by* HY PESKIN

> ## Artifacts

Pad to the Bone

They began as flimsy padding sewn into players' shirts and evolved, over the next 100 years, into the body armor that sits upon the shoulders of Giants (and Lions and Bears), making big men look even bigger

c.1920

1925

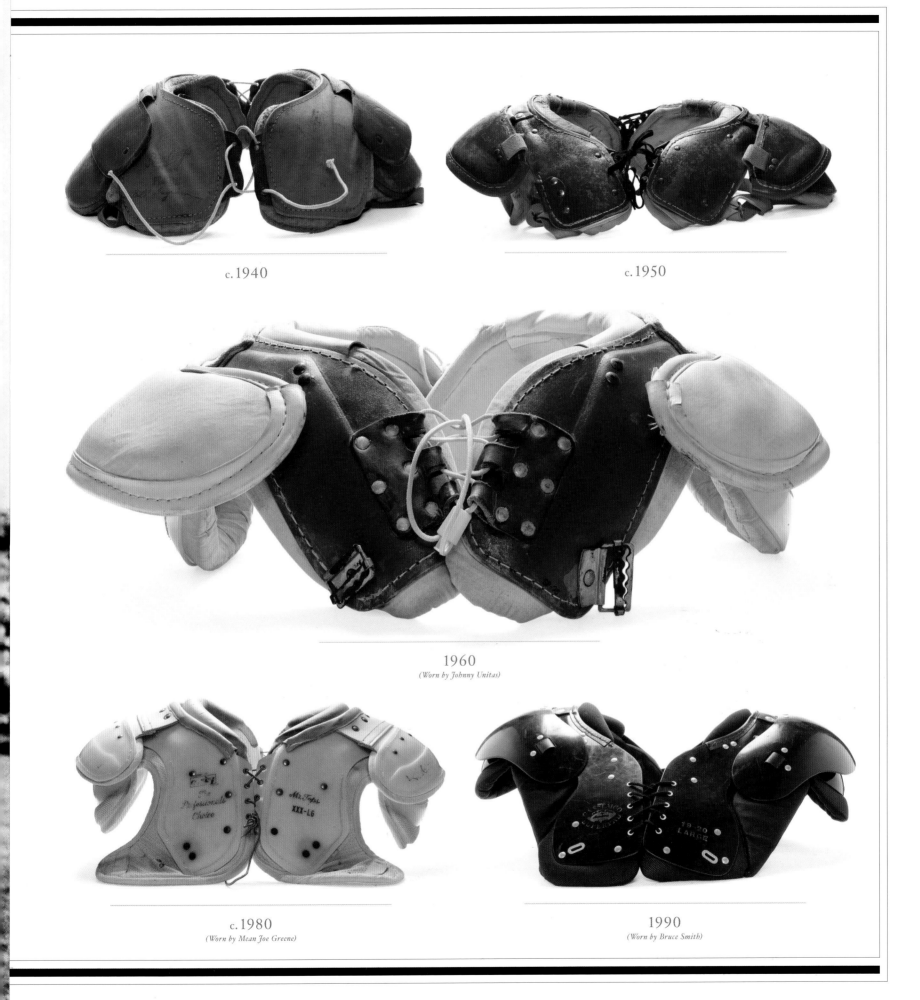

c.1940

c.1950

1960
(Worn by Johnny Unitas)

c.1980
(Worn by Mean Joe Greene)

1990
(Worn by Bruce Smith)

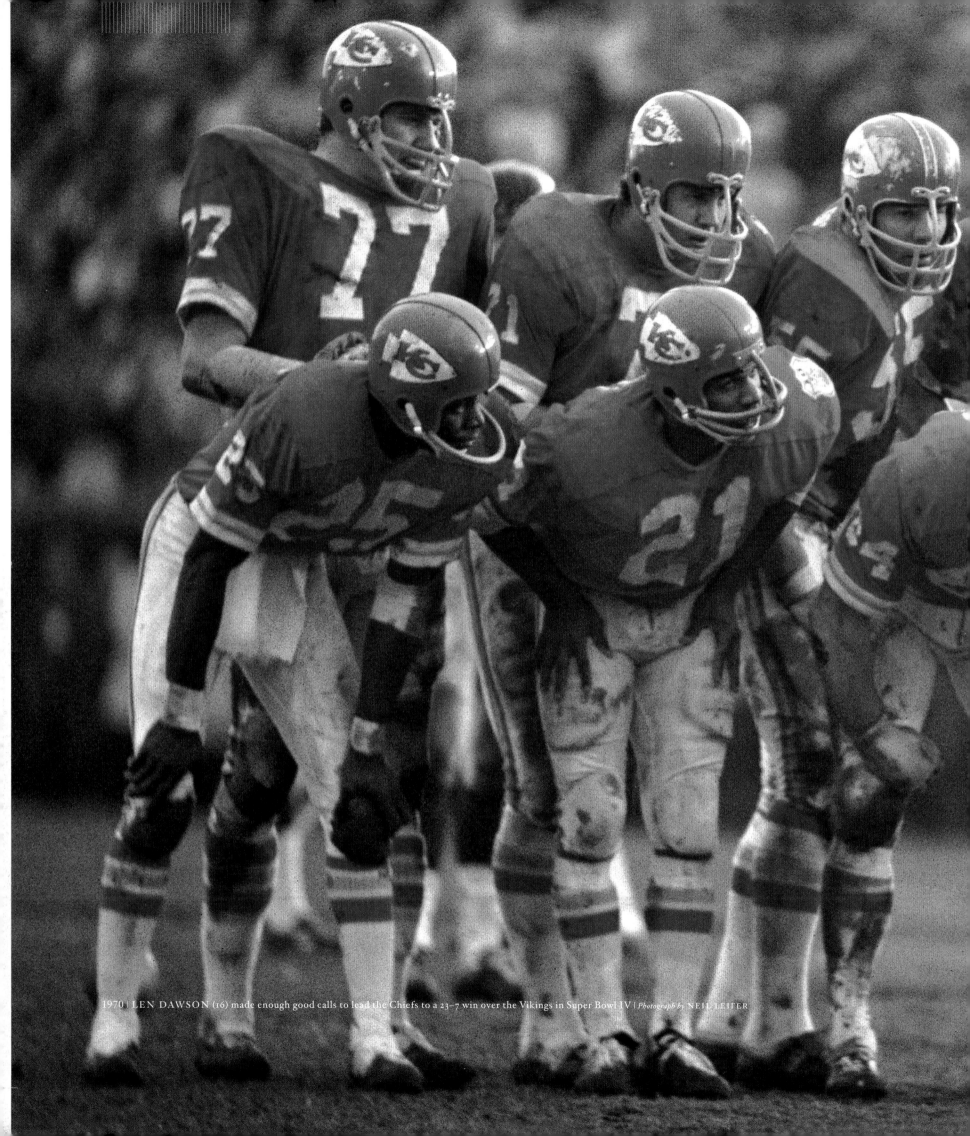

1970 | LEN DAWSON (16) made enough good calls to lead the Chiefs to a 23–7 win over the Vikings in Super Bowl IV | *Photograph by* NEIL LEIFER

1988 | JOE MONTANA did the dirty work while burying the Vikings in the NFC playoffs | *Photograph by* ANDY HAYT

1965 | THE BROWNS took the shine off Packers golden boy Paul Hornung (5) in the NFL title game, but Green Bay won | *Photograph by* VERNON BIEVER

NO PAIN, NO GAIN

BY MICHAEL SILVER

Offensive linemen do thankless work in the trenches, trying to outhit and outwit opponents. Few fans even know their names, but no team goes far without them. —from SI, DECEMBER 8, 2003

IF A QUARTERBACK IS A TEAM'S FIELD general, the offensive linemen are its special-ops forces, doing the dirty work under the cover of darkness. They may be among the smartest men on the field, yet they also absorb the most physical abuse. "Figure that one out," says Philadelphia Eagles guard John Welbourn, a fifth-year player who has a B.A. in rhetoric from Cal. "We're getting hit 70 times a game, and we watch more film than almost anyone else. To do our jobs you have to have a specific mental makeup."

Offensive linemen value smash over flash, for there's no other position in major professional sports that is less glamorous. For every Jerry Kramer, whose block allowed Green Bay Packers quarterback Bart Starr to plunge to victory in the Ice Bowl 36 years ago, there are 10 guys like Bubba Paris, whose faulty pass protection helped land San Francisco 49ers quarterback Joe Montana in the hospital after the Niners' 1990 NFC Championship Game loss to the New York Giants.

"We are the grunts," says New Orleans Saints center Jerry Fontenot, a 15-year veteran. "It's a thankless job because you get no glory and a lot of blame. My motto my entire career has been, No news is good news. But I will say this: Playing offensive line teaches you the principles of [teamwork] because if you're on your own program, the team won't be able to function."

From a fan's perspective, Fontenot is a relic from the blissful era of team stability. When he joined the Bears as a third-round draft pick in 1989, Chicago's starting line had been intact for four seasons. The arrival of unfettered free agency soon made such cohesiveness difficult. It also fattened the wallets of scores of lucky linemen, especially left tackles, who protect the blind side of righthanded quarterbacks.

If you're wondering why NFL franchises can no longer sustain success over an extended time, look no further than the trenches. "Your best lines are the ones that stay together, and those are usually the best teams," says Minnesota Vikings tight end Hunter Goodwin. "There are so many calls to be made, so many times when you need to intuitively know how the guy next to you is going to react, that continuity is

everything." It's hardly surprising, then, that the Kansas City Chiefs, who after their 28–24 win over the San Diego Chargers on Sunday owned an NFL-best 11–1 record, had started the same five linemen for 28 consecutive games, the longest such streak in the league in 11 years. Yet how many of these names (left tackle Willie Roaf, left guard Brian Waters, center Casey Wiegmann, right guard Will Shields and right tackle John Tait) do you recognize?

Life is a bitch in the trenches, especially when you're facing a player like three-time Pro Bowl guard Ron Stone of the 49ers. "When Ron starts barking," San Francisco offensive tackle Derrick Deese says, "that means he's whupping your ass." Stone is especially prone to dogging weak defensive linemen, known among their offensive counterparts as "clerks." To Stone and his linemates, the word conjures more laughs than Kevin Smith's cult film of the same name. "A clerk," says Jeremy Newberry, the Niners' Pro Bowl center, "is someone who should be taking the groceries to your car." Adds Deese, "We also call them 'limo riders'—we ought to send a limo to pick them up and make sure they get to the stadium on time."

The sentiment that inspires Stone's canine outbursts is one to which all offensive linemen can relate. "Defensive players celebrate over every little thing," he says. "Hell, we need to start celebrating. Even the little stuff gets me barking these days."

Offensive linemen view themselves as cerebral behemoths who know more about what's happening on the field than anyone in uniform other than the quarterback. In the seconds before he snaps the ball, the center (and, to a lesser extent, his fellow linemen) must decipher coverages, blitz packages and fronts in order to call the appropriate blocking assignments.

"We have to dabble in everything," Welbourn says. "That's why I think that to be a good offensive lineman, you have to be a bit of a Renaissance man." An avid reader (among his current selections: *Way of the Peaceful Warrior* by Dan Millman) and traveler (he's planning a trip to China in the off-season) who rides customized choppers, Welbourn would seem to fit an eccentric definition of the well-rounded man. The same can be said of his friend Kyle Turley of the St. Louis Rams, a heavily tattooed tackle who surfs, plays guitar and is an aspiring actor.

"It's not like we're a bunch of dumb guys, like most defensive linemen," Stone says. "Instead of just lining up in the three-gap and hitting the hole, we have to know what's going on." . . .

SIZE MATTERED for 6'3", 318-pound Nate Newton, but it took more than sheer bulk to earn the Cowboys guard six trips to the Pro Bowl.

> Artifacts

> **Artifacts**

Going to Extremes

Not all balls were created equal in the NFL's early days, so elaborate efforts were made to subject the equipment—and the elements—to some measure of control

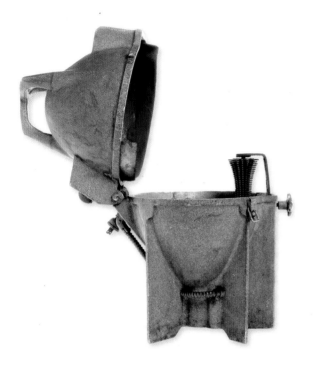

IN THE '50s, long before domed stadiums or heated benches, the league tried using massive ball-warmers to counter the cold—an experiment that was soon abandoned.

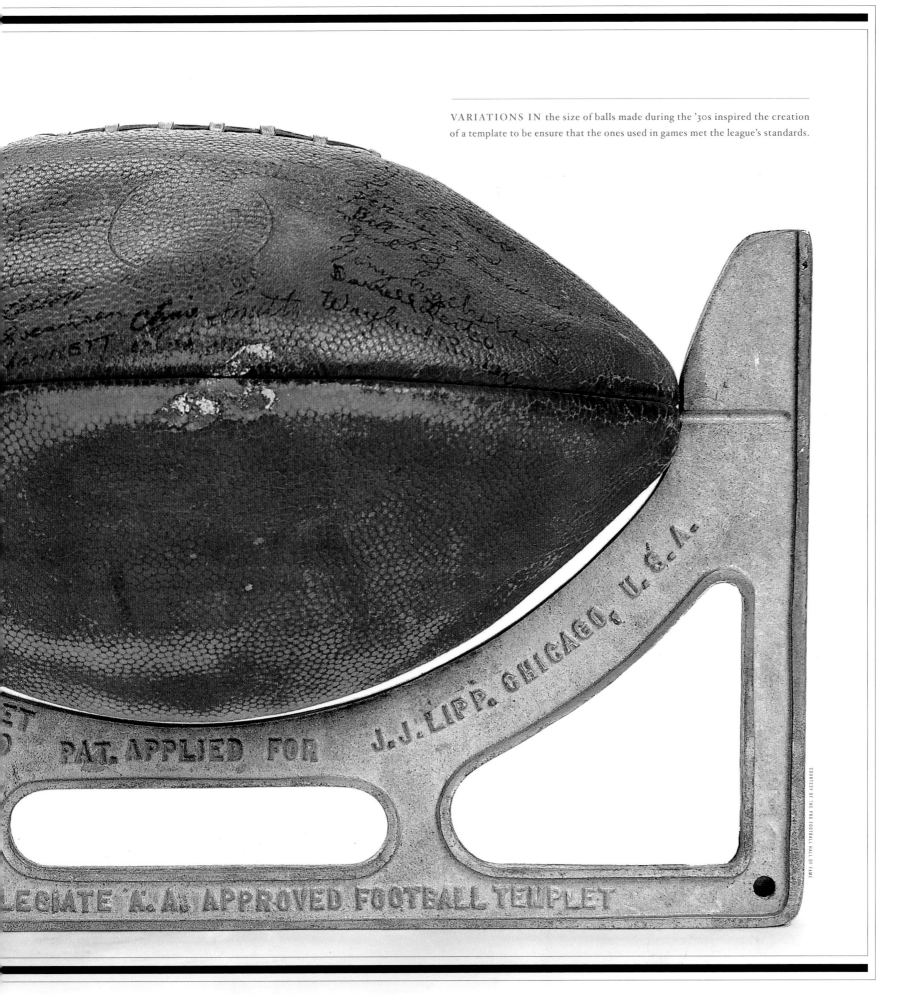

VARIATIONS IN the size of balls made during the '30s inspired the creation of a template to be ensure that the ones used in games met the league's standards.

> **SI's TOP 25** *The Linebackers*

JACK LAMBERT
Photograph by TONY TOMSIC

JUNIOR SEAU
Photograph by MARC SEROTA

MIKE SINGLETARY
Photograph by JOHN BIEVER

TOMMY NOBIS
Photograph by VERNON BIEVER

DERRICK THOMAS
Photograph by JEFF JACOBSEN

SAM HUFF
Photograph by NEIL LEIFER

LAWRENCE TAYLOR
Photograph by SPORTSCHROME

TED HENDRICKS
Photograph by AL MESSERSCHMIDT

RAY LEWIS
Photograph by TOM DIPACE

BOBBY BELL
Photograph by RICH CLARKSON

CHUCK BEDNARIK

BOBBY BELL

DERRICK BROOKS

TEDY BRUSCHI

NICK BUONICONTI

DICK BUTKUS

HARRY CARSON

BILL GEORGE

JACK HAM

TED HENDRICKS

SAM HUFF

JACK LAMBERT

WILLIE LANIER

RAY LEWIS

KARL MECKLENBURG

RAY NITSCHKE

TOMMY NOBIS

DAVE ROBINSON

JOE SCHMIDT

JUNIOR SEAU

MIKE SINGLETARY

LAWRENCE TAYLOR

DERRICK THOMAS

ANDRE TIPPETT

DAVE WILCOX

1978 | STEVE LARGENT, a Seahawk for 14 years, held six major career receiving records when he retired in 1989 | *Photograph by* MANNY MILLAN

1954 | BROWNS RECEIVER Ray Renfro was wide open for this TD catch in Cleveland's 56–10 win over the Lions in the NFL title game | *Photograph by* RONNY PESKIN

GETTING THERE THE HARD WAY

BY RICK TELANDER

The Broncos were postseason goners until John Elway engineered what will forever be known as The Drive.

—*from* SI, JANUARY 19, 1987

H AVE YOU EVER BEEN mean to a nice old dog? Did you sit there with a tail-wagging mongrel at your knee and kindly offer him a meaty bone, and at the last instant, just after his head lunged forward but before his teeth clicked shut, pull the bone away? Have you? Just for fun?

Then you've been John Elway, the Denver quarterback who yanked the bone from the mouth of the Cleveland Browns, 23–20 in overtime, for the AFC Championship in Cleveland Stadium on Sunday. No, let's clarify this metaphor. Elway didn't just pull victory from the Browns' mouth. He ripped the thing from halfway down their throat. The game was over. The Browns had won. It was that simple. But then, with 5:32 remaining and Denver trailing 20–13, Elway led his team 98 yards down the field on as dramatic a game-saving drive as you'll ever see. It was the way Elway must have dreamed it while growing up the son of a football coach.

The drive, one of the finest ever engineered in a championship game, had been performed directly in the Browns' faces. There was no sneakiness about it; John Elway had simply shown what a man with all the tools could do. It was what everybody who had watched him enter the league as perhaps the most heralded quarterback since Joe Namath knew he could do. One was left with the distinct feeling that Elway would have marched his team down a 200-yard- or 300-yard- or five-mile-long field to pay dirt.

Playing on unfriendly turf, generating offense where there had been precious little before, Elway ran, passed, coaxed and exhorted his team in magnificent style. Finally, with 39 seconds left and the ball on the Browns' five-yard line, he found Mark Jackson slanting over the middle in the end zone and hit him with a touchdown bullet. After that, the overtime was a mere formality. Elway took the Broncos 60 yards this time, giving Rich Karlis field goal position at the Cleveland 15-yard line and a sweet piece of advice: "It's like practice." Karlis's 33-yard field goal, his third of the afternoon, cut through the Browns like a knife.

Only a few minutes earlier, back in regulation, when the home team still had that big seven-point lead, nobody in the delirious Cleveland throng could have imagined such a nightmarish turn of events. Browns wide receiver Brian Brennan sure looked to be the hero of this game when he made it 20–13 by twisting safety Dennis Smith into a bow tie on a 48-yard touchdown reception from quarterback Bernie Kosar, a play that seemed destined to go straight into the NFL archives. The Broncos misplayed Mark Moseley's ensuing knuckleball kickoff and downed it at their own two-yard line. There was no way they were going to drive 98 yards and score a touchdown. No way. On its two previous fourth-quarter possessions Denver had moved just nine and six yards, respectively.

The Broncos' only touchdown drive had been a mere 37-yarder set up by a fumble recovery. Otherwise they had gotten only two short-range field goals from Karlis. To make matters infinitely worse, Elway had a bad left ankle, and the Browns had a ferocious, yapping defense. And straight behind them was the Dawg Pound, the east end-zone section where fans wore doghouses on their heads and bellowed for their Dawgs to treat Denver like a fire hydrant. Even from this distance the Broncos were amazed at the insane howling of the Pound. "I just waited for guys to run into me," said left tackle Dave Studdard. "I could not hear."

It didn't matter. Using hand signals and a silent count, Elway began moving his team.

Now, the image of John Elway conjures up different things to different people. Some see a hot-tempered California beachboy who runs all over the place throwing heaters without ever winning big games, at least not on the road. Others see a still-developing athletic prodigy, surrounded by not too much offensive talent, almost ready to take his place at the table of Graham, Unitas and Staubach. His teammates see a leader. "In the huddle after that kickoff to the two he smiled—I couldn't believe it—and he said, 'If you work hard, good things are going to happen,'" says wide receiver Steve Watson. "And then he smiled again.". . .

GIMPY BUT INDOMITABLE, Elway gained 20 of the 98 yards with his legs, including a nine-yard scramble that set up the game-tying toss to Jackson.

1949 | LEATHER HELMETS like this one worn by the postwar Chicago Cardinals sent players into battle with relatively little protection | *Photograph by* DAVID N. BERKWITZ

1925 | THE BEARS knew Red Grange (far right) would be a big draw in Chicago and paid him accordingly (about $12,000) for his first pro game | *Photograph by* UNDERWOOD & UNDERWOOD

2003 | THE JETS' Curtis Martin (28) needed four-wheel drive to make headway against the Steelers in New Jersey | *Photograph by* DAVID BERGMAN

LORD OF THE REALM

BY JOHN ED BRADLEY

Hard to believe, but Deion Sanders was as good as he often—and loudly—proclaimed himself to be. — *from* SI, OCTOBER 9, 1995

YOU SEE THE MAN IN jewelry, black shades and a do-rag. His mouth is running. Deion Sanders seems anything but a figure to replicate in marble, a statue for the ages. But put him in a football uniform and point out a man for him to cover, and he is the best defensive back in football, among the best of all time.

This is not news to everyone—certainly not to the quarterbacks who dread throwing in his direction, to the receivers who are routinely shut down by him, to the coaches who wish he were on their team. "You play him, it's just intimidating," Rams receiver Isaac Bruce says. Bruce was a rookie last season when he faced Sanders. "I kept thinking he'd come out ragging me or talking a lot of noise. You know the image he has. I didn't have any nightmares beforehand, but during warmups when I saw him come out on the field, it was hard to look at anything else."

This is what a receiver sees when he stands across the line of scrimmage from Deion Sanders: a man somewhat thick of hip, cut square and hard on top and long-limbed. His stance is like nobody else's. He crouches low. On occasion he will hold his hands in front of his face, his fingers tickling invisible piano keys. To some he resembles Bruce Lee set to unload on a pile of bricks. One foot is thrown back, set there until the ball is snapped and he throws it forward to deliver what he calls a quick jam. A quick jam is just that: a fast and artful check on the receiver, designed to slow him and upset his rhythm. Sanders can pin you to the line. He can stop you cold.

Bruce, the greenhorn, looked at Sanders across the line, and what he saw was something altogether different from what he had been expecting. Standing there as mute as a scarecrow in a deep winter field, Sanders was smiling. He was smiling as if he and Bruce were old pals, linked to each other in ways too profound and mysterious to describe. "That's all he did," Bruce says. "Smiled. Then later I'm running my routes, and instead of giving me a hard time, he's kind of coaching me. He's saying, 'Look, you need to stay low when coming out of your cuts, so I won't be able to tell where you're going.' "

Bruce took Sanders's advice, but alas, he finished the game without any catches while Sanders was covering him. Bruce wasn't the first receiver to get dusted by Sanders. Nor was he the first to come away feeling slightly awed by the experience. The man was even better than his hype: quicker, faster, stronger. And, on top of everything else, Sanders could coach. To offer advice to your own teammates is one thing; to give it to the player you are engaged in trying to stop reveals a self-confidence that is downright spooky. Sanders told Bruce how to beat him; then he went out and beat Bruce anyway. "When we played him last year, we talked about not even bothering to throw his way," says New Orleans Saints receiver Michael Haynes. "It was part of our game plan to keep the ball away from him. There were routes we wouldn't run toward Deion. He can take away that much."

"He takes one third to one half of the field away from the offense," says Flipper Anderson, the former star Rams receiver. "Think about it," Bruce says, in perhaps the most succinct evaluation of Sanders's importance to a defense. "Deion doesn't need any deep help. He doesn't need any help behind him like other defensive backs do. I mean, that alone tells you how good he is. It's like he's this lone man out there. He's on an island, protecting that island all by himself."

And nobody's going to get close. . . .

IN HIS prime Sanders could shut down big receivers, fast receivers and even big, fast receivers such as the Cardinals' David Boston.

2003 | TITANS RECEIVER Justin McCareins had a meeting of the minds with Panthers linebacker Mike Caldwell (59) and safety Jarrod Cooper | *Photograph by* BILL FRAKES

2007 | CRUNCH TIME arrived for Chiefs quarterback Trent Green in the person of the Colts' Robert Mathis (98) and Bo Schobel | *Photograph by* AL TIELEMANS

MUDDIED
BUT UNBOWED

BY JEFF MacGREGOR

This was the season he was going to ascend to the cosmology of one-name stars. This was the year his team was going to the Big Show. This was the year it all fell apart...yet Keyshawn Johnson continued to shine. —*from* SI, NOVEMBER 8, 1999

KEYSHAWN JOHNSON has to stick his head up over the knot of reporters in front of his locker and yell to the clubhouse guy for a jockstrap. This happens almost every day before practice. Then, still talking— seamless, uninterruptible—he goes back to the questions. Can you? Will you? Did you? Minicamp, training camp, preseason, real season; this is New York, so there are always questions.

For the past three years he's had answers, too, answers that are by turns funny and incendiary and smart, audacious or elusive or self-congratulatory, right, wrong, contradictory, contentious, sweet, sour, true and false. He is a 72-point banner headline waiting to happen. His relationship with the press is as vivid a part of his life as the game itself. Sometimes it *is* the game.

He'll crack you up. He'll piss you off. He'll ask better questions than you do. If he doesn't think a question makes any sense, he'll repeat it. Slowly. Like he's doing a lab at Berlitz. He'll stand there holding his practice pants—so small they look as if they came from Baby Gap but threaded with that long, swashbuckler's belt—and repeat the question. Eventually it makes sense to no one, not even the blushing knucklehead who asked it. Sometimes he ignores the question and answers a question nobody thought to ask. Sometimes he asks *and* answers the questions. Man!

He is as brash and self-referential as the young Ali, minus the poetry; as irritating and engaging and confounding to conventional wisdom as Ali before he leveled Liston. Is he really as good as he says he is? "I can hurt you all over the field." Who can be that good? "I can carry this team." No-body's that good! "Reinvent the position"? Who would even say this kind of stuff!

He stands 6' 3". He weighs 212 pounds. He trains year-round for his day job as a wide receiver for the New York Jets: weights, plyometrics, running. Off-season he runs in the California hills. Or he runs those famous stairs that lead down to the sand at Santa Monica beach. There are hundreds of them. This might take a couple of hours. He runs until he's ready to puke. Matinee-idol jock millionaire, and he's about to puke in front of tourists on their way to the Santa Monica pier. This is when James Strom, his strength coach, tells him to run some more. That way, when reporters call Strom to ask what sort of shape Keyshawn is in, he can answer in simple declarative sentences: "Nobody works any harder. Pound for pound he's up there with the strongest guys in the league."

If Keyshawn Johnson didn't exist, the press would have to create him. The way he created himself.

THIS IS how he works: Under a sky as high and hot as scalded milk, Keyshawn is running patterns on a practice field at Hofstra University, catching long, elegant passes.

He comes off the line of scrimmage like Walter Brennan. For the first three steps he's all crotchet and fuss and pistoning forearms, his big feet flapping. Then on the fourth step his feet are under him again, so he unfolds himself and he's daddy longlegs now, football fast, going, pumping—he plants one of those size-13 shoes, cutting, fakes, fakes again with a shake of the head that seems like an angry denial, pumping, going. Part of him is headed upfield now, and the other part isn't. You can see him from every angle at once, a cubist painting of a man running, and the ball is in the air, drilling an arc into those hands as big and soft as oven mitts.

During the worst of this unseasonal heat wave it feels as if you're wearing clothes made out of steel wool, but Keyshawn is running flat-out up the sideline, going deep, hitch and go, over and over—fast, as if he's chasing something. Or something's chasing him. . . .

THE TOP draft pick in 1996, Johnson averaged 13.6 yards per catch and almost 1,000 receiving yards over the next three seasons.

2003 | BROWNS DB Chris Akins gave Antwaan Randle El a new way of looking at things during the Steelers' 36–33 wild card win | *Photograph by* BOB ROSATO

2005 | RUBBING HIS nose in it, Atlanta safety Cory Hall reached in and rattled the cage of Philadelphia center Hank Fraley (63) | *Photograph by* DAVID BERGMAN

> SI's TOP 25 *The Defensive Linemen*

MEAN JOE GREENE
Photograph by GEORGE GOJKOVICH

ALAN PAGE
Photograph by NFL

HOWIE LONG
Photograph by LOUIS DELUCA

MERLIN OLSEN
Photograph by JOHN G. ZIMMERMAN

BOB LILLY
Photograph by TSN

BRUCE SMITH
Photograph by ELSA HASCH

CHARLES HALEY
Photograph by JAMES D. SMITH

DOUG ATKINS
Photograph by NFL

BUCK BUCHANAN
Photograph by RICH CLARKSON

REGGIE WHITE
Photograph by JEFFREY PHELPS

DOUG ATKINS

ELVIN BETHEA

BUCK BUCHANAN

WILLIE DAVIS

ART DONOVAN

CARL ELLER

LEN FORD

MEAN JOE GREENE

CHARLES HALEY

DAN HAMPTON

DEACON JONES

HENRY JORDAN

BOB LILLY

HOWIE LONG

GINO MARCHETTI

LEO NOMELLINI

MERLIN OLSEN

ALAN PAGE

WARREN SAPP

LEE ROY SELMON

BRUCE SMITH

ERNIE STAUTNER

RANDY WHITE

REGGIE WHITE

JACK YOUNGBLOOD

2006 | PADDING SEEMED superfluous for Joey Porter as the sculpted Steelers linebacker came off a Super Bowl and Pro Bowl season | *Photograph by* MICHAEL O'NEILL

2006 | WITH A face mask fronting a mouth guard, the dental health of Chargers defensive back Antonio Cromartie looked very bright indeed | *Photograph by* JOHN BIEVER

PEYTON'S PLACE

BY MICHAEL SILVER

On a rainy night in Miami, Peyton Manning reached the promised land, leading his Indianapolis Colts to a win in the biggest game of all. —*from* SI, FEBRUARY 13, 2007

IN PURSUIT OF A VICTORY THAT would recast his reputation, his heart racing with anticipation, Peyton Manning called the boldest and most controversial audible of his career. Twelve days before he would face the Chicago Bears in Super Bowl XLI, he stood up in a meeting room at the Indianapolis Colts' training facility and delivered an unpopular decree to his teammates who had gathered to talk logistics before their weeklong trip to South Florida. Colts president Bill Polian, one of the NFL's most autocratic executives, had announced that there would be restrictions on visitors to the team's hotel in Fort Lauderdale but that players would be free to spend time with family members and other guests in the confines of their own rooms. This unnerved Manning, who essentially threw out Polian's play for one more to his liking. "I don't think we should let *anyone* up in the rooms," Manning told the stunned group of players and coaches. "This is a business trip, and I don't want any distractions. I don't want any crying kids next to me while I'm trying to study."

That Manning would get his way was a foregone conclusion—Indy has been Peyton's Place since his arrival as the No. 1 pick in the 1998 draft—but grumblings of dissent still filled the room. "People were saying, We're grown-ass men. We'll make those decisions for ourselves," recalls veteran cornerback Nick Harper. "But, you know, it turned out all right."

Hyperfocused to his heart's desire, Manning was at his Super Sunday best in leading the Colts to a 29–17 victory before 74,512 fans at Dolphin Stadium. In earning MVP honors and shedding his can't-win-the-big-one tag (as did Indy coach Tony Dungy, who defeated his close friend and former assistant Lovie Smith in a matchup of the first two African-American head coaches in Super Bowl history), Manning overcame a sketchy start and seized control of a sloppy game in a driving rainstorm. Yet the seven-time All-Pro needed plenty of help to claim the Colts' first championship since their move to Indianapolis in 1984, and relying on his teammates to provide it was another sign of his maturation. A year after appearing to criticize his offensive linemen following a painful playoff loss to the Pittsburgh Steelers, Manning now understands, as he said a few hours after the game, "that everybody's got to do his part, and you have to trust them all to do that."

Late that night fans were dancing in the streets of Indy thanks to players such as rookie halfback Joseph Addai (143 rushing and receiving yards), his backup Dominic Rhodes (21 carries, 113 yards) and second-team cornerback Kelvin Hayden, whose 56-yard interception return for a touchdown with 11:59 remaining provided the game's final points. By then Manning had solved Chicago's formidable defense with a barrage of underneath passes and timely run calls while Indy's far less heralded D had repelled the Bears attack.

Before Manning (25 of 38, 247 yards, one touchdown) took hold of the game, the Bears mustered one show of offensive force. A 52-yard run by halfback Thomas Jones set up Rex Grossman's four-yard touchdown pass to wideout Muhsin Muhammad, giving Chicago a 14–6 lead with 4:34 left in the first quarter. But Indy pulled ahead before halftime on the first of three Vinatieri field goals and Rhodes's one-yard scoring run. With a 16–14 lead, the Colts' increasingly energized defenders were confident the game was theirs.

"Once we got the lead, we knew," said Harper. "We wanted to put the ball in Grossman's hands. Now I can say what I'd really felt all week: We'd seen the film, and we knew there was no way in hell they were going to beat us in the passing game."

The game had been over for an hour and a half before Manning finally showered. He didn't leave the locker room until after midnight, when the rest of his teammates had already boarded buses that would take them to the victory party at their hotel. At 30, after so many years spent in the spotlight—that's life when you're the son of football icon Archie Manning—he had finally earned the bling that would validate his status as one of the game's enduring elite, and he wanted to get the party started.

The rain drenched Manning as he left the stadium and walked briskly toward the last of the buses. A few steps behind, his older brother, Cooper, looked back and, worried that Archie might be left behind amid the confusion, yelled, "Dad! Come on! We've got to go!" Archie picked up the pace, but it proved unnecessary. There, waiting at the bus's front door, was Peyton, smiling like a newly crowned champion. As his teammates could have attested, there was no way in hell that bus was leaving until the quarterback was good and ready. . . .

REMAINING CALM amid a storm, Manning won the big one at last by keeping the Bears off balance and rallying the Colts to a lead they wouldn't surrender.

1950 | MARION MOTLEY (76) helped break pro football's color barrier when he signed with the Browns in 1946; his shoes, which carried him to the rushing title in '50, are in Canton. | *Photograph by* AP *(opposite)*

from CRASH COURSE | BY PETER KING

SI October 30, 2000

FOUR DECADES AGO THE NFL fullback was a force, in many cases more of an impact player than the halfback and wideouts were. Jim Taylor, with the Green Bay Packers in 1962, was the last pure fullback to win the league rushing title. For most of today's spread offenses, plodding is out and speed is in, making fullbacks as anonymous as linemen. Which is, in effect, what most of them are. "I see the position as being a glorified guard," says Jacksonville Jaguars fullback Daimon Shelton.

"Name me five or six fullbacks," says Bill Parcells, the New York Jets' director of football operations. "See? You can't do it."

On about 80% of the snaps the traditional fullback in today's game either delivers a crushing block on a defender who's usually much bigger, while leading the running back into a hole, or he shields the quarterback from a pass rusher. On maybe 15% of the plays the fullback is an option in the passing game, though often only a safety valve. On 5%—and this is generous when you consider that five of the 31 first-unit fullbacks do not have a rushing attempt through the first eight games of this season—they carry the ball.

"Besides being unselfish," says Denver Broncos running backs coach Bobby Turner, "a fullback has to be mentally tough. On 60 out of 70 plays he has no chance to touch the ball. On a great day he might have five balls thrown at him, and three won't even be catchable. But he's got to come back on every snap and be positive, put his face in there, slam into people, pick up blitzes, pick up linemen. Then after doing all that, he's quietly taking his shower and the halfback's got the microphones and minicams in front of him."

They are anonymous, and they are sore, and they'd better like it that way. "The only thing I could compare us to are the crash-test dummies flying around in those cars, crashing at 30 mph," says Cincinnati Bengals fullback Clif (Totally) Groce.

"You see those big-horned sheep on *National Geographic* get about 10 yards apart, and they charge at each other and *bam*!" says the Atlanta Falcons' Bob Christian. "That's what we do." . . .

2002 | MIKE ALSTOTT'S job was to level whatever stood between him and the yardage that Tampa Bay needed. | *Photograph by* BILL FRAKES

> **Artifacts**

The Tops of Their Game

NFL helmets got bigger and stronger over the years, much like the players they protected

1919 | KNUTE ROCKNE

Massillon Tigers

1934 | GEORGE MUSSO

Chicago Bears

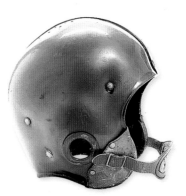

c. 1949 | SAMMY BAUGH

Washington Redskins

c. 1950 | LOU CREEKMUR

Detroit Lions

c. 1950 | JACK CHRISTIANSEN

Detroit Lions

c. 1956 | JOE PERRY

San Francisco 49ers

c. 1960 | CHUCK BEDNARIK

Philadelphia Eagles

1961 | BILLY HOWTON

Dallas Cowboys

1990 | BRUCE SMITH

Buffalo Bills

1970 | E.J. HOLUB, a five-time Pro Bowler at linebacker and center, banged heads in 127 games for the Chiefs and the Texans | *Photograph by* TONY TOMSIC

THE IMMACULATE RECEPTION AND OTHER MIRACLES

BY MYRON COPE

The Steelers dynasty was built on the most famous fluke play in NFL history, but who could deny that their long-suffering fans—and owner— deserved a little divine intervention?   —*from* SI, AUGUST 20, 1973

IN THE SPACE OF 40 YEARS, infants have grown to become Watergate plotters and beauty queens have retired to nursing homes. So 40 years is a long time, and unless you were one of us—that is to say, a part or partisan of the Pittsburgh Steelers, who after four desolate decades in the NFL won their first divisional title—you cannot possibly know the sweetness. Sweetness, did I say? More, it was the *ne plus ultra* of fruition when, as if to compensate for the lost years, everything fell into place.

I am 13, walking, sometimes skipping down the hill to the foot of Bouquet Street, heading for the bowels of old Forbes Field. I pass through a narrow entrance into the vendor's hole, a dungeon furnished with two battered picnic tables and a few benches. No problem gaining entrance, for during the baseball season I had appeared regularly for the shape-up. On days when big crowds were expected and a great many vendors needed, boss Myron O'Brisky would force himself to look my way. He would sign, distressed at having run out of strong backs, and say, "O.K., kid, *soo-vaneers*."

But this was football season and I had no intention of working. An iron gate separated the vendor's hole from a ramp leading into the park to keep the no-goods among us from sneaking off to spend the day as spectators. I had learned that if I arrived early enough one of the bosses going

FRANCO HARRIS had to get past Raiders cornerback Jimmy Warren to score on the miracle catch that put the Steelers into the AFC championship.

DONALD J. STETZER/PITTSBURGH POST-GAZETTE/AP/WIDE WORLD PHOTOS

to and fro would leave the gate unlocked for a few moments. I would dash through, sprint clear to the top of the ballpark in rightfield and hide in a restroom. It would be 2½ hours till the ballpark gates opened, but I passed the cold mornings memorizing the rosters I had torn from the Sunday sports section. At 11 a.m. I would be in position for a front-row space amid the standing-room crowd.

We came knowing we would suffer. Picture, if you will, a chunky man named Fran Rogel who, if given a football and told to run through a wall, would say "On what count?" It is 1955, and the Steelers have a splendid passer named Jim Finks and a limber receiver named Goose McClairen. They also have Fran Rogel at fullback and a head coach named Walt Kiesling, who in training camp a few months before cut a rookie named John Unitas. A big, narrow-eyed German, Kiesling wears the expression of a man suffering from indigestion and has the view that there is only one way to start a football game. On the first Steelers play from scrimmage, Sunday after Sunday, rain or shine, he sends Fran Rogel plowing up the middle.

The word having gotten around, the enemy is stacked in what might be called an 11-0-0 defense. From the farthest reaches of Forbes Field 25,000 voices send down a thunderous chant, hoping ridicule will dissuade Kiesling: "Hi-diddle-diddle, Rogel up the middle!" And up the middle he goes, disappearing in a welter of opponents battling like starved wolves

for a piece of his flesh. From his seat in the press box Art Rooney—the Chief—tightens the grip on his cigar till his knuckles whiten. Never has he interfered with a coach. But he has absorbed all he can bear, so for the next game he furnishes an opening play. "Kies," he tells the coach, "we are going to have Jim Finks throw a long pass to Goose Mc-Clairen. That's an order."

McClairen breezes into the open field, there being nobody in the 11-0-0 defense remotely concerned about him, takes Finks's pass at a casual lope and trots into the end zone. The touchdown is called back. A Steelers lineman was offside. After the game Rooney confronts the offender, only to learn from the poor fellow that Kiesling ordered him to lurch offside. "If that pass play works," Kies hissed at the lineman, "that club owner will be down here every week giving us plays." A philosophical man, the Chief never again makes the attempt.

So you see, it was not that we always had the worst talent in the league. On the contrary, Jim Brown used to say, "You'll usually find a way to beat the Steelers, but on Monday you'll ache as you haven't ached all season." Heroes we always had. From Johnny Blood to Bullet Bill Dudley (who as a rookie complained of being driven from the huddle by the whiskey on his teammates' breath) to Bobby Layne and John Henry Johnson, we had football players to cheer, but usually not enough of them.

THE BALL richocheted off the shoulder pads of Tatum, who was covering Fuqua, and fell miraculously into the hands of Harris at the 42-yard line.

2008 | PINPOINT PLACEMENT didn't yield a TD for Cardinals receiver Anquan Boldin, who was ruled out-of-bounds against the Giants | *Photograph by* JOHN BIEVER

2003 | BRINGING THE pylon to heel, Bengals back Jeremi Johnson tallied a touchdown that put Cincinnati ahead of Kansas City | *Photograph by* JOHN BIEVER

> **SI's TOP 25** *The Defensive Backs*

LARRY WILSON
Photograph by TONY TOMSIC

MIKE HAYNES
Photograph by RICH CLARKSON

CLIFF HARRIS
Photograph by RUSS RUSSELL

DARRELL GREEN
Photograph by LAWRENCE JACKSON

PAUL KRAUSE
Photograph by AP

RONNIE LOTT
Photograph by AL MESSERSCHMIDT

RODNEY HARRISON
Photograph by TOM DIPACE

ROD WOODSON
Photograph by JOHN BIEVER

MEL RENFRO
Photograph by TONY TOMSIC

HERB ADDERLEY
Photograph by TONY TOMSIC

HERB ADDERLEY

DICK ANDERSON

CHAMP BAILEY

LEM BARNEY

MEL BLOUNT

BOB BOYD

WILLIE BROWN

JACK CHRISTIANSEN

KENNY EASLEY

DARRELL GREEN

CLIFF HARRIS

RODNEY HARRISON

MIKE HAYNES

KEN HOUSTON

PAUL KRAUSE

DICK (NIGHT TRAIN) LANE

RONNIE LOTT

ED REED

MEL RENFRO

DEION SANDERS

EMLEN TUNNELL

ROGER WEHRLI

LARRY WILSON

WILLIE WOOD

ROD WOODSON

LET'S HAND IT TO HIM

BY RICK TELANDER

Jerry Rice's dedication to his craft made him the most prolific receiver in the game's history. —*from* SI, DECEMBER 26, 1994

THE BEST? ❧ HE'S HERE, in blue tights and red windbreaker, bitchy as a diva with a headache. ❧ The best ever? ❧ He's right here, sitting at his locker, taking off his rain gear after practice, edgy as a cat in a sawmill. ❧ Around him swirls the clamor of big men winding down, messing around, acting like fools. Two bare-chested linemen lock up and start to grapple, rasslin' and snorting like trash-talking sumos. Other players laugh, but not the best ever. "Guys," he says irritably. "Hey, guys!" Someone could get hurt.

The two wrestlers slowly come apart, his voice bringing them to their senses. They've heard the voice before; it's their fourth-grade teacher scolding them for rolling spitballs. It's the voice of San Francisco 49er Jerry Rice, the best wide receiver ever to play football. The 6' 2", tightly braided coil of nerves, fast-twitch fibers, delicate grasping skills and unadulterated desire is setting such high standards for the position that they will probably never be approached again, and he can't stand distractions while he works.

Rice does not fool around. Ever. He works so hard at his conditioning that during the off-season he virtually exits his body and studies his physical package the way a potter studies clay. "I mess with it," he says. "I like to do different things to motivate myself. I set goals and go after them."

As a rookie in 1985 he came to the 49ers at a muscular 208 pounds, but now he weighs 196. He is so lean that you wonder if he's sick. He likes to mess with his body fat, wants it to know that he is its master. For Rice, fat is a cornerback in man coverage with no safety in sight, a minor and ultimately irrelevant nuisance. Eschewing dietary fat, he got down to 189 a year or so ago, but the weight loss was too much. His starved body was literally eating up his muscles. His trainer ordered him to start eating things like ice cream.

"Under four percent body fat and I don't feel good," Rice states. "I'm a health-food fanatic, but getting that low really hurt my performance. I'm at 4.8 percent now, and I feel good." Well, not really *good*. Not the way you or I might feel good if we knew that not only were we certifiably the best receiver in the history of football but, perhaps, the greatest offensive player ever. That argument can be made. Rice already has more receiving touchdowns and more total touchdowns than anyone in NFL history. He has more 1,000-yard seasons than any other receiver, more touchdown catches in a Super Bowl and more consecutive games with a touchdown reception than anyone.

Was he this good in college? Imagine, for a moment, that it's September, 1984, and you are in sweltering Itta Bena, Miss., watching Mississippi Valley State coach Archie (Gunslinger) Cooley direct his Satellite Express offense, with quarterback Willie Totten flinging passes to a senior wideout named Rice, who races out of a stacked receiver formation that looks something like a Motown chorus line. In the first four games of that season Rice caught 64 passes for 917 yards and 12 touchdowns. As a junior he caught 24 passes in one game, an all-division record. He left school with 18 NCAA 1-AA records. Yes, he was good.

Rice never missed a game in college, nor has he missed one as a pro. Since he joined the 49ers the team has gone 126-45-1 (best in the NFL during that period) and won two Super Bowls. And at the seemingly advanced age of 32, he is still in his prime.

Early this season he talked about his compulsion to prove himself, to never let up even for an instant out of fear that everything might come apart. He had started at the bottom, and he could be back there in a heartbeat; people would forget him, and if that happened . . . would he even exist?

Afield, as in life, Rice is evasive. He almost never takes a direct, crushing blow after catching a pass. He controls his body like a master puppeteer working a marionette. A one-handed grab here, a tiptoe up the sideline there, an unscathed sprint through two closing safeties when it seems decapitation is imminent.

"I don't think I've ever seen him all stretched out," says 49ers quarterback Steve Young of Rice's ability to avoid big hits. Rice jumps only when he has to, and unlike almost all other receivers, he catches passes in mid-stride and effortlessly continues running, the ball like a sprinter's baton in his hand. It's almost certain that no one has run for more yardage after catching the ball than Rice. Though he's not particularly fast, Rice has a fluid stride and a sudden burst that, as Young says, "is a speed you can't clock."

And the hands. Clad in gloves, the hands are so supple and sure that last year they snared a touchdown pass by latching onto the *tail end* of a fading ball. "That was not giving up on the ball," explains Rice. Sounds simple. In reality it's like grabbing the back end of a greased pig. . . .

RICE MADE 11 catches—including this one-hander—against the Bengals in Super Bowl XXIII.

1957 | THE LIONS' Yale Lary, kicking against the Browns in Briggs Stadium, was the NFL's leading punter three times | *Photograph by* MARVIN E. NEWMAN

1967 | A REF'S WHISTLE from the title game known
as the Ice Bowl (temperature in Green Bay: -13°, with a
windchill of -46°) ended up in Canton. Bart Starr (15) ended
up in the end zone on a quarterback sneak that gave the
Packers the win over the Cowboys | *Photograph by AP (right)*

DICK (NIGHT TRAIN) LANE came up in an era when cornerbacks were still called defensive halfbacks. He played a style of football that was born of poverty and desperation. Years later his technique would acquire the catchy name "bump and run," but when he came into the NFL, in 1952, his approach was as elemental as the game itself. Lock on a receiver, rough him up as he makes his way down the field, try to knock him off his pattern, and if he still caught the ball, take his head off.

Lane, who died last week of a heart attack at age 73, was the most feared corner in the game. A big guy at 6' 2" and more than 200 pounds, he was known for the Night Train Necktie, a neck-high tackle that the league eventually banned. "I've never seen a defensive back hit like him," Packers Hall of Famer Herb Adderley once said. "I mean, take them *down*, whether it be Jim Brown or Jim Taylor."

If Lane had been only a roughneck, he wouldn't have put together a 14-year career, which he spent with the Rams, the Chicago Cardinals and the Lions, nor would he have ended up in the Hall of Fame. He had speed, phenomenal leaping ability and great hands. Ironically, when he broke in with the Rams, they switched him from receiver to defense because they thought he had trouble holding on to the ball. He made 14 interceptions in his rookie year (in only 12 games), still the NFL single-season record.

I used to see him from time to time at Hall of Fame gatherings, always smiling, always friendly. "Until he got sick [with diabetes] a few years ago, he'd always be back here for the Hall of Fame weekend," says John Bankert, the Hall's executive director. "He'd always ask me the same thing, 'Is there anything I can do to help?'

"One of the last times I saw him, he said, 'You know, sometimes I feel that I'm not worthy of being here.'"

No one was worthier than Night Train Lane. . . .

1961 | LANE'S TRADEMARK necktie tackle, part of his bruising repertoire, was later banned by the NFL. | *Photograph by* BETTMANN

1997 | PACKERS GUARD Adam Timmerman got a wet kiss after Green Bay beat the 49ers to reach the Super Bowl | *Photograph by* TONY TOMSIC

1964 | BROWNS RECEIVER Gary Collins was swarmed by Cleveland fans after scoring one of his three touchdowns in the title game | *Photograph by* TONY TOMSIC

1959 | GIANTS QUARTERBACK Charlie Conerly needed two men to protect him from Colts end Gino Marchetti in the title game | *Photograph by* NEIL LEIFER

CODE OF HONOR

BY GARY SMITH

Responding to the 9/11 attacks the only way that made sense to him, Pat Tillman did the unthinkable: He walked away from his NFL career and joined the Army Rangers. — *from* SI, MAY 3, 2004

EVEN BEFORE THE WORLD Trade Center incinerated, even as a linebacker at Arizona State in 1996 and '97, Pat Tillman would lie in bed on the eve of games and picture things that no teammate pictured. He'd envision the American flag and the blood that had been spilled for it and utter words that football players didn't, *shouldn't*, just hours before entering battle. "There's more to life than football," he'd say. "I want to contribute to society and help people."

Then came the phone call one September morning from his brother Kevin, an infielder in the Cleveland Indians organization—*Turn on your TV, right NOW, Pat!*—and the image on the screen of the second airliner hurtling into the second glass tower full of human beings. The next day came Pat's interview with NFL Films, when he said, "I play football, and it just seems so goddam—it *is*—unimportant compared to everything that's taken place. . . . My grandfather was at Pearl Harbor and a lot of my family has gone and fought in wars, and I really haven't done a damn thing. . . . "

"We're worthless. . . . We're actors," Pat had muttered as he watched events on a locker room TV the day after the attacks. What did people expect him to say a half year later when, like his brother, he decided, at age 25, that he couldn't do what every other pro athlete did—keep playing ball and leave it to others to do what had to be done? What did they expect him to do—*talk* about it?

Relatives tried to persuade the Tillman boys to change their minds. Their father—Pat Sr., a lawyer and former college wrestler at San Jose State who had told his sons long ago that he regretted not having followed the family footpath into service—knew that dissuasion would be futile. One day Pat pulled a chair around the desk of then Cardinals coach Dave McGinnis and said, "Mac, we've gotta talk," walking away later that day and leaving Mac to do all the talking to the media.

The Tillman brothers made the Rangers. Pat's reward was a pay cut from the $1.2 million a year the Cardinals would have paid him to $17,316. "I can't stop smiling," his old college coach, Bruce Snyder, told *The Miami Herald* at the time, "and I'm not really sure why."

The news [that Pat Tillman was killed in action in Afghanistan] whistled through America's soul and raised the hair on the back of its neck. It tapped into people's admiration, their awe, their guilt. In a country where no civilians have been asked to sacrifice anything and where even the cost of the war is being forwarded to their children and their children's children, a man had sacrificed the biggest dream of all: the NFL. During World War II, 638 NFL players served and 19 died in action, but no well-known U.S. professional athlete in a quarter century had volunteered for service, and none had perished since Buffalo Bills lineman Bob Kalsu in Vietnam in 1970.

Memorials sprang up overnight, balloons and flowers and teddy bears and notes left, and a man stood before a photo of Pat outside Sun Devil Stadium—home to ASU and the Cardinals—and blew *Amazing Grace* through his bagpipes. Scholarships were founded, and the Cardinals announced that a plaza outside their unfinished new stadium will carry his name. Before its story had even been written, SI had received 103 letters about Pat's sacrifice. Pat had no need for the fuss. But the people did. At last they had a face to grieve.

"There is in Pat Tillman's example," said Senator John McCain of Arizona, "in his unexpected choice of duty to his country over the riches and other comforts of celebrity, and in his humility, such an inspiration to all of us to reclaim the essential public-spiritedness of Americans that many of us, in low moments, had worried was no longer our common distinguishing trait."

The mist of human motive is as dense as the fog of war. Pat Tillman may have died in the Middle East last week because it was the only place on earth where he could get a good night's sleep. But anytime a man listens to his inner voice, refuses to wall it off with all the mortar and bricks that his culture can possibly offer, it's a moment to stand in wonder as well as to weep.

Elizabeth McKenrick, the wife of 4th Ranger Training Battalion Commander Terry McKenrick, couldn't help herself last Friday. As a rule she shields her three children from newscasts about the war because otherwise she knows that the next time their dad is shipped from Fort Benning, Ga., to the Middle East, she won't stand a chance of convincing them he'll return home. But when she saw the TV report about Pat Tillman, she called her nine-year-old to her side. "Listen," she said. "Listen to the story of what this man did." . . .

1973 | THE PACKERS defense was very much in its element against Vikings running back Chuck Foreman in Green Bay | *Photograph by* JOHN BIEVER

1964 | JIM BROWN led the NFL in rushing in eight of the nine years he played for the Browns, and retired in his prime, at 30 | *Photograph by* NEIL LEIFER

2004 | A BOMB intended for Washington's Rod Gardner (87) was defused by a pack
of Green Bay defenders headed by Nick Barnett (56) | *Photograph by* DOUG PENSINGER

SUPER BOWL - NEW YORK GIANTS - DEFENSIVE CALL SHEET - JANUARY 28, 2001

VS. REGULAR

SERIES Reduce Stir 22K
50/50 - Tilt FZ   I = LT
 • (St) Ov Snk Swill 1Lk •
 • (St) Under Shunk 63

1ST DN (St) Ov Snk 63
SL Run   Eagle Storm
(20 In) Reduce Op Smoke Sp. 1
         (St) Ov Ed 3

INC Reduce Tilt 63 Zone X
SL Run (St) Ov Snk Stud 1Lk
        (St) Ov Ed 3

2ND 7+ Und Stir 22K
SL Pass Reduce Knife 43 / 63
(Scrn)   Tilt FZ
         (St) Ov Ed 3 (Tom)

2ND MD Reduce Knife 63
50/50   Under Shunk Zone X

2ND SHT Ov Ed (Knife) 3
Run   Reduce Tilt Zone X

VS. TIGER

Series Cyclone Dog 1
Hvy Run Under 63
         Open Storm
         Ov Snk 63

1st (St) Ov Ed 4
50/50 Over Whip You 1Y
       Ov Ed 3
       Ov Snk 63

2nd 7+ Ov Ed Stir 2B
Pass   Reduce Op Smoke Sp. 1
       (RS) Strong FZ
       (St) Ov Ed Combo 4

U / GREY

Vandy - (St) Ov Snk Stud 1Lk
         Ov Snk 63
         Ov Ed 3
         Under 1/2 7, 63

Hvy - Over 6 Match
        Backer Storm
        Over Hammer O

VS. 1ST / 2ND PASS

3W	E
50/50	Under Me 63
Und 1/2 7	Und 1/2 7
Ov Combo 4, 3	Und Sam 1
	Ov Ed (Combo) 3, 6

BASE VS. 3W	1ST & 2ND DOWN
	E
Flex 78	Under Me 78
Flex Change	Flex Change
BA	Nickel Dog 1
Dime Viper	Dime Viper
Bear Peel 1	
Dime Dog 1	Tiger - Flex Change/78
	Nickel Dog 1

BACKED UP Eagle Storm / Open Storm
         Over Sink 63
         Tilt FZ
         (St) Ov Ed 3
         Reduce Knife (Combo) 22K, 63

4 MINUTE (St) Ov Snk Stud 1Lk
         Eagle Storm
         Hvy-Over 6 Match
         Reduce Tilt 7, 63
         Cyclone Dog 1

2 MINUTE

Patient - Begin w/ a Run. Screen on 2nd Long. 3WR 2x2-Alert ZSeam - H ✓ Down. Trips=HiLoWk. Ch-78, HiLoStr or H. Regular-Bunch/ Levels concepts.

Rush 58 Str, 78
3-2 Rush 52W
Rush Change / 54
BA
Double Dog 1
Drop Kathy

3RD DOWN SUB

	3W	4W	Reg	E
3RD LNG	30 Blast 1	30 Peel 1	Rush 58 Str	Rush 58 Str
	(RS) Bear Nickel Go 1	30 Hound 1	Strong FZ	BA
	30 Rush Str 58 Str	Rush Change	Rush 52W	Bear Peel 1
	Rush 52W	3-2 Rush 52W	Bear Peel 1	30 Blast 1
	3-2 Rush Auto	30 Gut O		
	30 Ray 55			
	Rush 55 (30 Peel)			
3RD REG	Double Dog 1	Strong FZ	Rush 52W	Bear Hk 78
	Rush 52W	30 Blast 1	30 Near FZ	30 Peel 55
	BA	3-2 Rush Change	3-2 Rush 78	Rush 52W
	Bear Hk 78	30 Trap 52W		
	Rush Change			
3RD MED	Bear Peel 1	Rush 52W	Rush 52W	Max Blitz O
	Flex Change	Rush 78	Flex 78	Dime Viper
	30 NR FZ			Under Me 52W

Tiger

MA-

MA

3rd 3-4
Rush 52W
30 Hound 1
Rush Change

GOAL LINE

1st Goal Line Banjo

2nd Goal Line Banjo

3rd Goal Line Banjo

REG. RED ZONE

HIGH RED Reduce Knife/Stir 22K, 63
         Ov Ed (Tilt) 3, 4

± 15 Ov Ed (Tilt/Knife) Red 2
       Flex (Tom) Red 2
       (Vandy) Ov Ed Red 2

PRESSURE Eagle Storm
         Tilt FZ / Cyclone Dog 1

MUST STOP Reduce Hammer O
         Ov Snk Stud Up OLk
         U - (Ok) Sink Stud Up OLk

SUB RED ZONE

HIGH RED (Sub) Flex/Rush Change 52W

± 15 Flex/Rush R52
       3-2 Rush R52

PRESSURE 30 Blast 1
         BA
         Strong FZ

2 PT PLAY 30 Gut O
         (Sub) Flex R52

MUST STOP Max Blitz O
         30 Gut O

SHORT YARDAGE

REG- Ov Snk Stud 1Lk
       Cyclone Dog 1

3W- (BS) Flex Change, 71Y
       Under 1/2 7 (Combo)

U- Hvy-Backer Storm
      Over Hammer O
      (Ok) Sink Stud 1Lk

TIGER- Und Sam 1
         Und 1/2 7

JUMBO- SY Under Zone the Set

2001 | RAVENS QUARTERBACK Trent Dilfer (8) could have used a peek at the Giants' play sheet (left) before facing their defense in the Super Bowl | *Photograph by* CHUCK SOLOMON

TIME AND PUNISHMENT

BY PHIL TAYLOR

*No position is more physically taxing than running back, where
the best are often finished not long after they get started.*

—*from* SI, NOVEMBER 4, 2002

WHETHER THEY ARE contact-seeking battering rams like Pittsburgh's Jerome Bettis or slippery change-of-direction artists like Marshall Faulk of St. Louis, all running backs absorb the kind of abuse usually reserved for guys who have missed one too many payments to their loan shark. "You get pounded," says San Francisco 49ers running backs coach Tom Rathman, who spent eight of his nine years in the NFL as a Niners fullback. "You get pounded on every play. You're either carrying the ball and routinely taking three or four hits, or you're being asked to block some lineman or linebacker who's probably got at least 20 pounds on you. Everybody in this league takes his share of hits, but I don't think anybody takes them more consistently than backs."

Quarterbacks and kickers have more rules protecting them than the bald eagle. Linemen batter one another but usually from such close range that they don't have a full head of steam when they collide. Running backs get little relief from the rule book, and at the moment of impact with an opponent, one or both parties is often moving at high speed.

Not coincidentally, an NFL Players Association study that tracked rosters from 1987 through '96 found that the average career of a running back is 2.57 years, shorter than that of a player at any other position and nearly a full year shorter than the average for all NFL players. According to the report running backs have only a 6% likelihood of reaching their 10th year in the league. Among the 10 active running backs who have reached the 10-year mark, five are fullbacks and only two—Bettis and the Dallas Cowboys' Emmitt Smith—are their team's primary ballcarriers. Another feature back, the 49ers' Garrison Hearst, has also been in the league for a decade, but he missed two seasons because of a severe ankle injury and large chunks of two others with a torn left MCL.

It's far more common for running backs to go into early decline or retirement due to injury or the accumulation of blows. Gale Sayers played only 68 games before succumbing to knee injuries. Earl Campbell ran over defenders for six years and gained more than 1,300 yards in five of them before, at 29, his body seemed to suddenly lose its remarkable power. Two forgettable seasons later he retired. In 1998, at the age of 26, Jamal Anderson led the NFC in rushing while playing for the Atlanta Falcons, but four years and two torn ACLs later, he is out of football. The latest casualty is Terrell Davis of the Denver Broncos. After beginning his career with four phenomenal years, including a 2,008-yard rushing season in 1998, Davis played only 17 games over his next three years because of a series of knee, ankle and leg injuries, and in August he announced his retirement.

The ability of some running backs to withstand punishment over a long career while others flame out early is still a mystery, but there is evidence that the compact back tends to have more staying power than the big bruiser. Smith (5' 9", 216 pounds), who has missed only five games because of injuries in his 13-year career, and the Jets' Curtis Martin (5' 11", 205), who has been sidelined for only five games in eight seasons, are both relatively small, strong backs. So were Payton (5' 10", 202) and Barry Sanders (5' 8", 203), who had played 10 years and was still at the top of his game when he abruptly retired.

But regardless of size, the wise running back learns that there are two ways to increase his NFL life span—taking care of his body off the field and avoiding the full force of collisions on it. Even Bettis swivels his 256-pound frame enough to diminish the impact of defenders' blows. "I don't shy away from a lot of hits, but I shy away from hits I can't win," he says. "That's what people don't necessarily see. They see me run over one guy, but when there are two guys, they don't see me getting between them. I just try to be a little more elusive. I shield, I deflect blows. I go sideways. Longevity for big guys like me depends a lot on being able to slip away from that big, crunching blow."

When collisions are inevitable, it's better to be the hammer than the nail, as Rathman puts it. "Whenever possible you want to deliver a blow rather than absorb one," he says. "Backs who are always taking punishment and never giving it won't last long." . . .

DESPITE THE pounding he took, the bruising Bettis showed how a back could survive: by ducking some tacklers and making others pay a stiff price.

1969 | ALONE IN a crowd, the Jets' George Sauer (83) beat Baltimore's Lenny Lyles to corral a pass from Joe Namath during Super Bowl III | *Photograph by* WALTER IOOSS JR.

1989 | IN FULL FLIGHT, Eagles wide receiver Cris Carter snatched the ball before it could fall into the mitts of Redskins cornerback Brian Davis | *Photograph by* JOHN BIEVER

1966 | RUNNING BACK Lenny Moore and guard Jim Parker were a Pro Bowl duo for the Colts for six years | *Photograph by* WALTER IOOSS JR.

1967 | RAMS QB Roman Gabriel beat Willie Davis and the Packers on his way to earning the NFL's MVP in '69 | *Photograph by* WALTER IOOSS JR.

THE PATH TO POWER

BY AUSTIN MURPHY

There were many monumental events in the ascension of pro football, and prominent among them was appointment of a new commissioner who struck TV gold. —*from* SI, AUGUST 30, 1999

BERT BELL DIED OF A HEART attack on Oct. 11, 1959, leaving the NFL without a commissioner. Competent and well regarded, Bell nonetheless left behind a becalmed, underexposed league operating out of a four-person office in suburban Philadelphia and consisting of 12 teams with a dozen agendas. Attempts to replace him three months later were predictably strife-ridden. After 10 days of acrimony and 22 ballots at the Kenilworth Hotel in Miami, the owners finally agreed on a compromise candidate, the 33-year-old general manager of the Los Angeles Rams, Pete Rozelle.

As his destiny was being determined, Rozelle waited in a men's room off the hotel's lobby. "Pete told me that whenever someone came in, he'd walk to the sink and wash his hands," recalls former Cowboys president Tex Schramm.

The owners opted for this well-scrubbed wunderkind for one reason. "They all thought they'd be able to control him," says Schramm, who was one of Rozelle's closest friends. But Rozelle soon demonstrated that beneath his handsome tan and genial smile was a surprising amount of steel.

Halas learned as much early in Rozelle's tenure. In 1962 Halas broke a league rule and was summoned from Chicago by Rozelle to the NFL offices in New York City (where, as one of his first orders of business, the young commish had relocated NFL headquarters).

Halas suggested that Rozelle meet him at LaGuardia Airport. Came the stern reply, "I'll see you in my office at 10 o'clock, Monday morning."

Papa Bear did as he was told, and Rozelle fined him $1,000.

While it was important for the Boy Czar, as he became known, to establish his authority, that was merely a backdrop for what turned out to be his most important work: wedding his league to that great American pastime—television.

In the pre-Rozelle era clubs cut their own TV deals. The new commissioner's top priority was to persuade the owners of big-city teams to divide the television loot evenly among all owners.

Even though that sounded an awful lot like socialism, they agreed.

Next, Rozelle went to Congress and obtained an exemption to the Sherman Antitrust Act, enabling the league to sell all those TV rights collectively to a single network. Did Rozelle's business plan succeed? In 1962 teams received $330,000 apiece from television. By '64 the figure was $1 million. This year each team's TV cut will be $71 million. (The current deal, signed in 2006, yielded $3.75 billion per year in TV money to split up.)

In the summer of 1966 Rozelle was back up on Capitol Hill, lobbying the legislators for another antitrust exemption. This one was necessary for the NFL to merge with a contentious rival. Competing with Lamar Hunt's upstart AFL was proving fiscally ruinous for owners on both sides. At Rozelle's urging, the two leagues joined forces. Regarded at first as an anticlimactic oddity, the Super Bowl—it was known as the NFL-AFL Championship in its first two years, until '69—evolved into a national holiday of sorts. Nine of the 10 top-rated television shows of all time have been Super Bowls.

Permission to merge came at a cost: Congressmen from high-school-football-crazed regions spearheaded a law forbidding the NFL from playing on Fridays. "Thus, *Monday Night Football* was born," says Schramm, "because we had no place left to go."

Although CBS and NBC turned up their noses at the concept of pro football on Monday night—"What? Preempt *The Doris Day Show?*" asked an incredulous CBS executive—ABC took a chance in 1970.

In the '60s Rozelle also greenlighted NFL Properties as well as NFL Films, perhaps the most effective propaganda organ in the history of corporate America. But labor strife, franchise free agency and interminable lawsuits leeched much of the joy from the job for Rozelle, who retired in '89.

When he died of brain cancer seven years later, Rozelle was eulogized as a visionary, the first modern sports commissioner. Says Schramm, "He was the right guy with the right temperament at the right time."

Indeed, today's players owe their fortunes to those squabbling, old school owners and the compromise candidate they so thoroughly misjudged. The man they thought they would lead by the nose instead led their game to unimaginable wealth and popularity. . . .

ARCHITECT OF the modern NFL, the visionary Rozelle exploited the potential of television, pushed through a merger and presided with panache.

1994 | HATS OFF to L.A. Raiders linebacker Mike Jones for not flagging the official for a flagrant hold on this play | *Photograph by* RICHARD MACKSON

2004 | REDSKINS QUARTERBACK Mark Brunell couldn't tear himself away from the tenuous grasp of Detroit defensive end James Hall | *Photograph by* BOB ROSATO

THE DAY OF THE GAME

BY VINCE LOMBARDI WITH W.C. HEINZ

In this SI excerpt from his book, Run to Daylight!, *the great Packers coach chronicled the hours leading to kickoff on a football Sunday.* —from SI, SEPTEMBER 9, 1963

AFTER BREAKFAST ON the Sunday of the game, I look out the window and the sky is low and the air is loaded with moisture that has condensed into droplets on the shrubs and the lawn. Later, as I drive across the bridge, the first drops of rain hit the windshield. This is not going to help us a bit, but it is not going to help the other guys either. If we are going to take it right to them, I think, let's do it on the first play. Go to their strength, and if that's where we're going, our Brown Right-73 might be the one to open with. I like it because their middle linebacker is a great one and the sooner we go to work on him the better. It will give us at least two people on him. While I don't think we will discourage him, we should, if Jim Ringo and Ron Kramer both get good shots at him, force him to be a little concerned. That could help.

Except for half a dozen cars parked up by the entrance to the dressing rooms, the area is empty, and when I walk inside it is 10:25 and Hank Jordan is there, getting out of his jacket in front of his dressing stall. I look around the room at the stalls, each with the name card and jersey number on it, each with the gold helmet and shoulder pads above it, the gold pants hanging inside on the right, the green jerseys and blue warm-up sweaters on hangers on the left, the floor of each stall covered with six or eight or 10 pairs of football shoes at $23.50 a pair.

Earl Gros and Gary Barnes are undressing and in the trainer's room Ed Blaine and Ron Gassert, our two other first-year men, are having their left knees taped.

The veterans are coming in now—Forrest Gregg and Dave Hanner and Jim Ringo—and Hank Gremminger is getting out of his street clothes in front of his stall. "You give the doctor another workout?" Ringo is saying to Hanner.

"That's right," Hanner answers.

"What's the matter with you?" I ask Hanner.

"I felt hot and cold yesterday," he says.

"Did you go to the doctor?"

"Yes, sir. Then last night I went to bed at 8. I woke up at 10 sweatin' like anything, but I feel better today."

I hope you do, I say to myself, and I hope Jimmy Taylor walks in saying he feels better, too.

"How's Jim?" Ringo says. "Anybody know?"

"He says he had 101," Hanner says, "but he says he's gonna play."

I walk in the coaches' room. Red Cochran is holding his Packer blazer in his left hand and, with his right hand wrapped in white tape, brushing lint off it. Phil Bengtson is talking to Norb Hecker about UCLA's upset of Ohio State yesterday, and Bill Austin is on the phone checking with the airport about the weather. "It could be off and on," he says when he hangs up. "Light rains all afternoon. The wind is east-northeast, 10 to 12 knots."

"That's not the way the flags are blowing," Phil says.

"They're liable to be any way out there," Bill says.

I am at my desk now, thinking about Brown Right-73, our opening play. What I like about it is that it really goes to work on that middle linebacker. Ringo sets him up with a drive block for Ron Kramer, who releases from his tight-end spot and comes across and bull-blocks him. Taylor fakes up the middle and then takes that big 76. It's a tough block for Jerry Kramer on that 71, but if they give Paul Hornung any daylight and his thigh is all right he should go. Another nice thing about it, too, is that it is a good influence play on their left end. Forrest Gregg pulls across his face, making him think the play is going outside, and when it goes inside you've got that trap on him.

I look at our ready list, in its plastic envelope, the right formations on a 8 ×11 card, the left formations on the other side. I jot down half a dozen plays, any of which could be logical calls in our first sequence, depending on the result of our 73. "How's Taylor?" I say to Gene Brusky as I see him walk in.

"He had 101 last night, " Gene says. "It's normal this morning."

I walk out then and find Jim Taylor. "Jim?" I say "How do you feel? The doctor says you're going to be all right."

"I hope so," he says, and I hope so, too. He is one of those performers who has to be emotionally up and I'm hoping not only that the fever hasn't drained him physically but also that it hasn't defeated him psychologically.

"Jim? Bubba?" I say, and I get Ringo and Bubba Forester, our two captains, together. "If you win the toss, receive. If we have to kick off, take the north goal."

In the coaches' room I change into slacks and pull on a pair of white woolen socks and the ripple-soled coaching shoes.

"All right," I say, "I want the quarterbacks in here."

"Bart! Johnny Roach!" Cochran calls as the others leave.

THE PACKERS won only one game in 1958, the year before Lombardi arrived; three years later, they were the NFL champs.

When Starr and Roach come in, I sit down across from them. "Generally," I say, "your sweeps should be to your left. As far as your pitchout is concerned, I'd use 48 to the left side. When you're going for short yardage, you can expect the 6–1, so use those short-yardage plays we've been working on." They are intent and nodding. "Now for our first play let's try the 73. That's whether they're in the 6–1 or 4–3 or whatever they do. O.K.?"

"Yes, sir," Starr says.

They get up and leave. I put on my topcoat and transparent raincoat over it. I walk to the door of the dressing room and look at the players. They are now in uniform and wearing olive-green rain jackets and dark blue knitted skull caps. All of them are waiting.

"Let's go!" they shout, and they clap in unison and start filing out. Their cleats make the sound of hailstones hitting the concrete and, as I follow them out and look up, the rain, still light and hesitant, hits my face.

The stands are about two-thirds full. I pick a couple of tufts of grass and throw one up and then the other. The wind is not too strong and out of the northeast. If we lose the toss and have to kick off we will stay with the north goal.

In the far end zone Ringo and Forester are leading the calisthenics. Behind me I hear the roar from the stands and I turn and see the other team, in silver and white uniforms, coming out, down the ramp and out onto the field. I search the other side of the field until I find my counterpart, and I walk over.

"How are you," I say, and we shake hands.

"Fine," he says. "You?"

"All right," I say. "We drew a rotten day."

"We can't do anything about that."

"I'm sorry about the condition of the field, though," I say. "We've had rain most of the week, and they had a high school game here Friday night."

"I understand," he says.

"Well," I say, "good luck, and I'll see you."

"Thanks," he says. "The same to you."

As I turn I see that the referee is bringing over No. 56, that great middle linebacker of theirs. All week, day and night, he has been invading my thoughts, and now we shake hands. Ringo and Forester have joined us. Then I leave, and I'm aware that the light rain seems to have stopped.

"We won the toss," Ringo says when he and Forester come back. "We receive and they have the north goal."

"Good," I say.

I walk down to where Austin and Bengtson have the offensive and defensive lines facing one another. They are reviewing assignments. It is now 12:45. We have been out on the field for half an hour, so I send them in.

When they are all seated in front of their stalls, the other coaches and I go into our room and shut the door. It is 10 minutes to game time, and these three minutes that will follow, with just the squad members alone in the dressing rooms, is some-thing I started when I first came here in 1959. I was reaching for anything then that would give them a feeling of oneness, of dependence upon one another and of strength to be derived from their unity, so I told the captains that before each game this period would belong solely to the players. I do not know what is said in that room. I know that Ringo or Forester, or perhaps both, speak, and that if someone else wants to say something, he does. I know that at the end—and this is completely their thought and desire—they all join in the Lord's Prayer.

Someone knocks on our door and the other coaches and I walk back into the room. Now I have seven minutes, and I walk among them. I start out by going over the automatic we're going to use, the plays our quarterback will call on the line when he sees that the defensive alignment will negate what he called in the huddle. "We're going to receive," I say then, "and we've got the south goal. Remember that this club puts their speediest men as third men out from each side and they must be blocked. So let's take them out of there. Let's impress them, all of them, right on that kickoff. I don't have to tell you about the importance of this ball game. You know as well as I do that you're meeting today the top contender, and that no one can win it now but you. For two years these people have been on our necks, but if you beat them today you'll be making your job easier for the rest of this year. For you to do it, though, is going to require a top effort. You know that they think they can beat you, that they've said they will. That's why I say it's going to take a top effort.

"And now," I say, "I want all of you to know this. Regardless of the outcome today I'll still be proud of you."

"Let's go!" they shout, standing now, and they bring their hands together in unison again. "Let's go! Go!"

There is the roar of the crowd again, the faces and bodies bordering the walkway. There is the jam-up going down the ramp, and we stand, waiting amid the shouts, for the P.A. announcer to introduce our offensive team.

"At center," he says, the sound of his voice filling the air, and Jim Ringo runs out onto the field through the V formed by the cheerleaders and the Green Bay Lumberjacks' band, "Number 51—Jim Ringo! At right guard, Number 64—Jerry Kramer! At left guard, Number 63—Fuzzy Thurston! At right tackle. . . ."

We coaches then follow the rest of the squad out. The roar from the stands is beating down in waves around us and I am in the middle, crouching, with the squad pressing in around me. "Go out there and hustle," I tell them.

OUR KICKOFF-receiving team runs out. From the other sideline the other team is peeling out of its huddle. And now that nervousness which I have forestalled, which I have learned to control up to a point, starts to come. I watch the referee's arm come down and then I hear the whistle, and to my left that line of white shirts and silver pants and helmets moves forward and I see that ball rise. . . .

BART STARR, drafted in the 17th round in 1956, blossomed under Lombardi, leading the Packers to five NFL championships and two Super Bowls.

1960 | RAYMOND BERRY led the league with 74 receptions, 10 of them for touchdowns, including this grab against Washington | *Photograph by AP*

1975 | PRESTON PEARSON and Dallas caught Wally Hilgenberg (58) and the Vikings at the wire in an NFC divisional playoff game | *Photograph by* HEINZ KLUETMEIER

A GAME NO ONE SHOULD HAVE LOST

BY JOHN UNDERWOOD

In the muggy heat of Miami's Orange Bowl, two heavyweight offenses exchanged body blows for five quarters . . . and then staggered to the sidelines to watch as a kicker decided their fates in the greatest game ever played. —from SI, JANUARY 11, 1982

IT IS THE ONE GREAT IRONY of professional football that magnificent games such as San Diego's wonderful, woeful 41–38 overtime AFC playoff victory over Miami are almost always decided by the wrong guys. Decided not by heroic, bloodied men who play themselves to exhaustion and perform breathtaking feats, but by men in clean jerseys. Men with names you cannot spell, and the remnants of European accents, and slender bodies and mystical ways. Men who cannot be coached, only traded. Men whose main objective in life, more often than not, is to avoid the crushing embarrassment of a shanked field goal in the last 30 seconds.

There, at the end, in a moist, numbed Orange Bowl, still jammed with disbelievers after 74 minutes and 1,030 yards and 79 points of what San Diego coach Don Coryell called "probably the most exciting game in the history of pro football," was Dan Fouts. Heroic, bloodied Fouts, the nonpareil Charger quarterback. His black beard and white jersey crusted with dirt. His skinny legs so tired they could barely carry him off the field after he had thrown, how many? A playoff-record 53 passes? And completed, how many? A playoff-record 33? For a playoff-record 433 yards? And three touchdowns?

Ah, Fouts. The guy Otto Graham says activates "the greatest offense" in pro football history. (Outrageous comparisons are a dime a dozen around the Chargers these days.) Fouts sets records with every other breath. If he'd only pay his union dues, what a terrific fellow he would be. Fouts should have decided this game.

Or Kellen Winslow. There, at the end, his magnificent body battered and blued by a relentless—if not altogether cohesive—Miami defense, Winslow *had* to be carried off. Time after time during the game he was helped to the sidelines, and then, finally, all the way to the dressing room, the last man to make the postgame celebration. Staggering, sore-shouldered, one-more-play-and-let-me-lie-down Winslow, looking as if he might die any minute (the only sure way he could have been stopped), catching, how many? A playoff-record 16 passes? For a playoff-record 166 yards?

Winslow is listed as a tight end. The Dolphins know better. Like the 800-pound gorilla, Winslow plays just about wherever he wants to play: tight end, wide receiver, fullback, wingback, slotback. Even on defense, as Miami discovered when he blocked what would have been the winning field goal and thereby spoiled what Dolphin guard Ed Newman called—another drum roll, please—"the greatest comeback in the history of professional football." Winslow should have decided this game.

Or there, on the other side, Don Strock, the gutty, heroic Miami relief pitcher. Strock coming in with the Dolphins submerged at 0–24 and not only matching Smilin' Dan pass for pass, but doing him better than that for so long a stretch that it looked for sure the Dolphins would pull it out. Throwing for 397 yards and *four* touchdowns, and getting Miami ahead and into a position to win at 38–31, and then at the threshold of victory twice again at 38–38. In the end, breakdowns not of his doing cost Strock exactly what Newman said it would have been—the greatest playoff comeback in the NFL's history. "Strock," said Fouts, "was awesome." Strock should have decided this game.

Fittingly, all of the above helped make it what Fouts himself called "the greatest game I ever played in." (See? It's catching.) But, typically, none of them had even a bit part in the final scene. Overtime games almost always come to that because in overtime the objective shifts to a totally conservative aim: The first team close enough tries a field goal. Be cool, play it straight, pop it in. Thus, after a day-into-night parade of exquisite offensive plots and ploys, the final blow was a comparative feather duster, struck by a former 123-pound weakling in a dry, spotless uniform. After the haymakers that kept the old bowl rocking for almost four hours, it was a finishing jab that buckled the Dolphins. A tidy little 29-yard love tap that Rolf Benirschke put slightly right of center, 13 minutes and 52 seconds into overtime. . . .

WINSLOW (80) WAS helped to the sidelines repeatedly, then finally carried from the field before the Chargers beat the Dolphins in overtime.

1943 | SID LUCKMAN threw for seven touchdowns in this game against the Giants, a record that still stands | *Photograph by* CHICAGO TRIBUNE

1995 | STEVE YOUNG quarterbacked the 49ers to a 38–28 win over the Cowboys to advance to the Super Bowl—where they drubbed the Chargers | *Photograph by* V.J. LOVERO

EMMITT'S DOMAIN

BY S.L. PRICE

Stiff-arming his opponents and critics, Emmitt Smith became the leading rusher in NFL history. —*from* SI, NOVEMBER 4, 2002

SUDDENLY, LATE ON SUNDAY afternoon, he had nothing left to explain. It was all coming back: The line kept opening holes, and Emmitt Smith kept hitting them hard and gliding through, getting closer. Thirteen years ago he had vowed that he would get here, to this moment in football history, and now it was as if the intervening seasons had barely left a mark. He spun. He juked. He ground out yard after yard against the Seattle Seahawks, 55 in the first quarter alone, each step taking him closer to Walter Payton's NFL rushing record, each step taking the sellout crowd at Texas Stadium back to his prime. Smith wanted it no other way, of course—for Payton's family, for the Dallas Cowboys, for himself most of all. He had struggled all season to find his game, feeling the city turning on him bit by bit, feeling for the first time the sting of words like *old* and *finished* and *selfish.*

All season Smith had tried to pretend that this didn't hurt. In his calmer moments before Sunday he would smile and take the long view, because Emmitt Smith is a religious man, and it is an article of his faith that each blessing brings a curse. Or he would just shrug, as if to say, *What can I do?*, for the Scriptures preach forbearance, and Lord knows he tries to live a righteous life. Still, there's a limit to his patience, and at times the shrug would turn to rage. Then the magnanimous Emmitt Smith was a 33-year-old bear swiping at the hounds at his heels, off and running about "couch potatoes" who "sit on their asses" and "idiots that've got these so-called sports shows" and "media chumps."

Running behind an injury-riddled line that's still learning a new blocking scheme, playing on a mediocre team for a city and franchise happy only with supremacy, Smith has this season entered that paradoxical zone inhabited by so many great athletes nearing endgame: Even as he was being celebrated for his march into history, teammates and coaches said he was not the force he used to be, fans insisted that his backup was better, commentators wondered if he was hurting the team. Nice career, Legend. Now isn't it time you stepped aside?

"You can just look at my age and say, 'Yeah, he's 33, he should go,'" Smith says. "Yeah, I am 33. But have I lost my step? Have I lost my vision? Have I lost my power? Have I lost my ability to make a person miss? If I answer yes to those questions, then you might be right. But don't tell me I should quit just because of my age. That's what makes this frustrating. You have to know who you are. I know who I am."

Indeed, long before Sunday, Smith could always look up from his desk at home and see a wood-carved reminder: EMMITT SMITH #22, WORLD'S ALL-TIME GREATEST RUSHER. Finally, against a notoriously porous Seattle defense, he set the notion in stone. Averaging only 63.9 yards entering the game— and needing 93 to break Payton's mark of 16,726 yards—Smith heard Seahawks defensive lineman Chad Eaton say during the coin toss, "You're not going to get it today on us," then flail helplessly as Smith uncorked his best effort of the year. By the fourth quarter, with Dallas down 14–7 and flashbulbs popping, he stood just 13 yards short of the record. Not for a moment did he seem surprised. The Cowboys' next two games are on the road. Smith wanted to grab history at home.

Yes, Smith knows who he is, and he knows *where* he is too. More than speed or power or balance, awareness has been his greatest asset. He's always been able to read the men shifting in front of him, anticipate where and when a hole would open, when to make that famous cutback. So it was: On first-and-10 at Dallas's 27-yard line Smith churned for three yards. On second down he took the ball from rookie quarterback Chad Hutchinson, cut left, found a seam, stumbled over a defender's arm, placed his right hand on the turf, kept his balance and kept on chugging until he had caught Payton and passed him by. Then Smith bounced to his feet, face alight, knowing without being told that the record was his.

On this day, he didn't look like a man about to go away; he won't do that until he's good and ready. Should anyone be surprised? Smith is, after all, pro football's ultimate survivor. Passed over by 16 teams on draft day in 1990, considered too small and too slow, he has outlasted all competition. Over the past five years at least a half-dozen backs have been more highly regarded than him: The list of those who began their careers after Smith, rose to stardom and then vanished is long and distinguished. Those are the vagaries in the life of an NFL running back—for everyone but Smith. He has endured concussions, bone chips, a broken hand. He is still here.

"By all the laws of nature and careers, he shouldn't be sitting in this locker room," says Cowboys owner Jerry Jones. "Every time I look over there, something inside me smiles." . . .

SMITH RAN for 1,773 yards in 1995, one of 11 thousand-yard seasons on his way to a new NFL career rushing record in 2002.

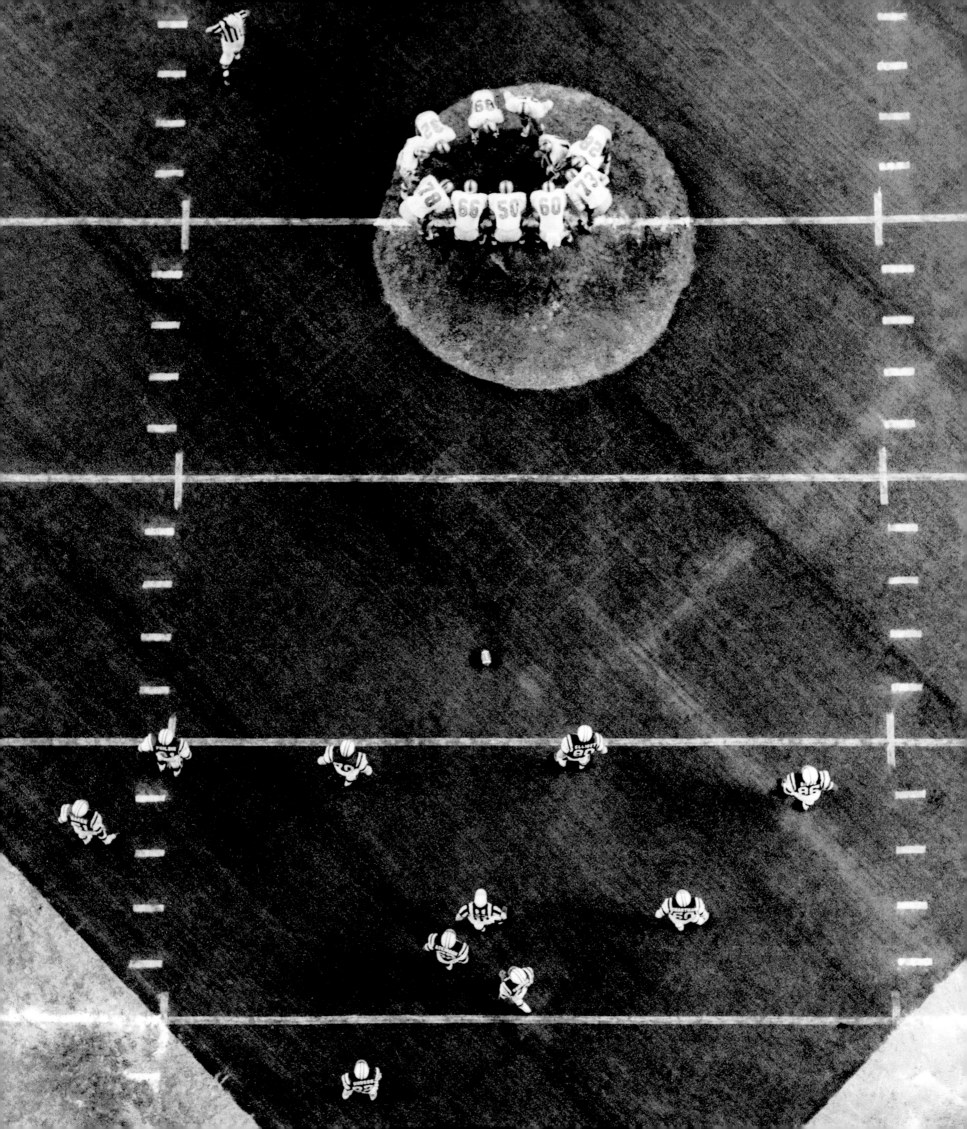

1968 | O MARKED the spot, the Astrodome pitching mound, where the Oilers offense huddled during a preseason game against the Jets | *Photograph by* NEIL LEIFER

1957 | HARD-NOSED FULLBACK Rick Casares bulled his way to five straight Pro Bowls with the Chicago Bears | *Photograph by* JOHN G. ZIMMERMAN

1999 TITANS QB Steve McNair paid a high price to reach paydirt against the Steelers. | *Photograph by* AL TIELEMANS

2007 | TAKING THE only available route, the Eagles' Brian Westbrook stepped lively over the Patriots defense | *Photograph by* DAMIAN STROHMEYER

2004 | END ZONE seats at Texas Stadium took a turn for the better when the Dallas Cowboys cheerleaders got behind their team | *Photograph by* BILL FRAKES

1895 | THERE WERE no shoulder pads in the game's early days; the only shock absorbers were a heavy canvas vest and jacket | *Photograph by* DAVID N. BERKWITZ

1930 | THE BEARS' backfield of Red Grange (left) and Bronko Nagurski was one of the league's great attractions | *Photograph by* AP

2003 | BALL-BEARING New England tight end Daniel Graham was on quite a roll after scoring against the Bills in Foxborough | *Photograph by* EZRA SHAW

1956 | RECOVERY EFFORTS by the 49ers (red) against the Browns were halted by the whistle of a vigilant ref | *Photograph by* HY PESKIN

2004 | STEELERS CORNERBACK Ike Taylor picked off a Tom Brady pass intended for the Patriots' Bethel Johnson in Pittsburgh | *Photograph by* JOHN BIEVER

1952 | IN FULL STRIDE, Giants defensive back Emlen Tunnell (opposite) clutched a ball ticketed for 49ers receiver Billy Wilson (84) | *Photograph by* BETTMANN

THE ULTIMATE TEAMMATE

BY CHARLES P. PIERCE

Though he was the indispensable element in three New England Patriots Super Bowl wins, quarterback Tom Brady was also the ultimate team player. —*from* SI, DECEMBER 12, 2005

AS IT TURNS OUT, PLATO WAS smarter than most football coaches, maybe even smarter than Bill Belichick. Back in the day, Plato realized that every athletic performance is an act of generosity, because of all the solitary effort it takes to make that performance possible. The generosity that begins in the rehearsal space blossoms on the stage. The generosity that begins on the practice field blossoms in the stadium.

Plato did not anticipate the National Football League, but what he wrote about athletes is more conspicuously true in football than it is in any other sport. Even the best quarterback—even, say, Tom Brady, a quarterback who rose from the Mel Kiper-ish netherworld of the sixth round of the draft to lead his team to three Super Bowl championships in four years—gets to actually play only once a week. The rest of the time is repetition, a Baltimore Catechism with sweat and collisions.

Thus is the life of any great quarterback. What makes Brady different is how vividly you can see not only the results of that work every Sunday, but also his innate ability to carry the logic of practice to the conclusion of the game. "I love seeing us get better," Brady says, "and I don't think you get better in games. The improvements come in practice." His high school teammates recall a practice dropback drill called the Five Dots, wherein the quarterback matches his steps precisely to marks on the ground, much in the way Arthur Murray once taught the clumsy how to waltz. Brady marked out a Five Dots course in his backyard and worked on it every day before school.

Sooner or later, though, to be complete in what you do and who you are, you have to leave the silence and walk toward the cheers. "I love it so," Brady says. "Just running out there in front of 70,000 people. . . ." And then his voice trails off, as though he's given explanation enough.

Brady has defined himself, always, as part of a team, and that's carried over into this year, when his celebrity caught up with his achievement. He re-signed for considerably less money than the market might've borne so the Patriots would have maneuvering room under the salary cap. When SI's Peter King asked him about it last February, Brady said, "Is it going to make me feel any better to make an extra million? That million might be more important to the team."

Moreover, it was Brady who insisted that his offensive linemen be his co-stars in a national credit card commercial, in which the linemen sit with Brady at dinner, in full uniform, and explain to him that they are the "metaphors" for the various features of the credit card. Adam Vinatieri is not one of the metaphors, but no player has benefited more from Tom Brady's generosity, nor has anyone—other than Brady himself—played a bigger role in Brady's success. It was Vinatieri's kicks that provided the winning margin in all three Super Bowls. And it is Brady's command of the final moments of a game that may one day enable Vinatieri to enter the Pro Football Hall of Fame. There has not been a relationship so mutually beneficial to a kicker and a quarterback since the last time George Blanda practiced alone.

These two men are defined—together—by their first two Super Bowls. On both occasions Brady led a drive that gave Vinatieri a chance to win the game with a field goal, thereby making it possible for Vinatieri to build a reputation as the greatest clutch kicker in the history of the NFL. Brady's résumé, of course, would be considerably less gaudy if Vinatieri had shanked those kicks. That reciprocity is where true generosity flowers. "He always gives us a shot," Vinatieri says.

The very best among us, like Brady, instinctively see the Platonic arc of it, and where it must lead. He has always known that solitary practice is worth it only if it leads to something that can be shared, with teammates, first, and then with the world, on the biggest stages, in the loudest arenas. "The perfect game's got to be for the highest stakes," Brady says, "and it's got to come down to the end. You don't remember the ones you win 35–12. You remember the ones you win 38–35, the dogfights. Those are the ones that are memorable. Who wants everything to come easily?" . . .

DEDICATED AND SELFLESS, Brady never lost focus or forgot his humble origins as a sixth-round pick, even after three Super Bowl victories.

2007 | WHO ARE those masked men? The 49ers' Jeff Ulbrich (53) and Derek Smith took a peek
at a pumped-up Monster Park crowd before facing the Ravens | *Photograph by* JED JACOBSOHN

1951 | A FROZEN FEW at Shibe Park saw Eagles linebacker Chuck Bednarik (60) and Browns receiver Dante Lavelli stretch for an Otto Graham pass | *Photograph by* AP

1968 | A CATCH by Colts receiver Willie Richardson even turned the head of Packers Hall of Fame defender Herb Adderley | *Photograph by* NEIL LEIFER

GETTING NOWHERE FAST

BY ROBERT F. JONES

They call it hard living, but it looked awfully easy when Kenny Stabler did it. —from SI, SEPTEMBER 19, 1977

THE BIG KNUCKLES bulge around a beaded can of beer, second of the morning though it is scarcely 9 a.m. "This is home," says Kenny Stabler. "I'll die here." The flat tone of the statement, issuing as it does from a face masked by a grizzled brown beard and mirrored sunglasses, raises questions. Does the premier quarterback of the NFL, the 1976 MVP, the star of Super Bowl XI, whose deft passes and clever calls eviscerated the Minnesota Vikings, mean that he's outgrown his hometown? That the rustic pleasures of Foley, Ala. (pop. 4,000) are beginning to pall? That he would die of boredom if he had to live here year-round?

Not a bit.

"I love this place," says Stabler, gunning the motor as he hits the edge of town. "It's got everything I'll ever need. Come on, let's get some beer and go for a boat ride."

A week with Stabler shot by like a long wet blur. Through it ran the sounds of Stablerian pleasure: the steady gurgle of upturned beer bottles, the clack and thunk of pool balls, the snarl of outboard motors, the whiny cadences of country music. At the end of it, anyone following in Stabler's wake would be ready for a body transplant: liver and lights, heart and kidneys, eardrums—maybe even a few new teeth.

It began in Memphis, where Stabler was expected to perform in the pro-am of the Danny Thomas-Memphis Classic. Stabler was waiting at the airport. He was, of course, in the bar. He had been there since noon. It was now close to 5 p.m. Surrounded by reeling pals, beautiful girls and an array of empty or partially drained glassware—beer bottles, Bloody Marys, Salty Dogs, Seven and Sevens—he grinned at a newcomer. "You're late," he exulted. "Thank God. Here"—he unwrapped his thick left arm from a petite blonde, who emerged like a bauble from the shadow of his armpit—"meet Wanda." She smiled demurely, then stuck out her tongue.

The next morning a caravan of Continental Mark Vs wound erratically through southeastern Memphis. "Where the hayull is the golf course?" snarled a Southern voice. "Danged if *Ah* know," answered another. "Turn on the goldurned *ayer* conditioner," gasped a third. "It's runnin' full blast, you knucklehead," was the response.

"Wayull, shore," continued Bear Bryant, as if he hadn't been interrupted. "Ah remember that boy. He looked like a good 'un but he always left his football game in some parked car the night before we played. Ah remember that Auburn game in. . . ." Bryant, Stabler's coach during his college All-America days at Alabama, was paired with Stabler for the pro-am. His deep, hoarse, mellifluous voice, eroded by hard living and the football wars of a quarter of a century, filled the car with meaningless magic, reminiscence. Stabler giggled like a schoolboy at the great man's mots.

Later, under a scorching sun, Stabler, his shots snaking into the rough, pleaded "migraine" and quit short of nine holes. "Hayull," grumped Bear in mock chagrin as Kenny was departing for the clubhouse. "Ah was gonna pull that one myself but you beat me to it."

STABLER IS now dining at a Gulf Shores squat-'n-gobble. Wanda at his side, before him his third Scotch of the meal and a heaping plate of scampi in garlic sauce. "Scotch and scampi," he crows between chomps. "I love 'em. Johnnie Walker Red. Namath drinks it. Sonny Jurgensen is a Scotch drinker too. Maybe all the great quarterbacks drink Scotch. And I love seafood, particularly these babies." (Munch, crunch, gulp.) "I told Pete Banaszak last season, just after we beat Pittsburgh in the opening game, that I'd eat scampi for 14 weeks in a row if it would guarantee us winning all our games." Like Proust's madeleine, the jumbo shrimp provoke a remembrance of the season past.

"We really didn't know what to expect from the Vikings in the Super Bowl. We knew they were an experienced team, disciplined, and well-coached at all levels, a no-nonsense bunch of guys, straight up, older than us but not necessarily wiser. We didn't think they'd add any new wrinkles for the Super Bowl, and we didn't plan to either. We'd stick with what had worked, what got us there. Some of our guys got up so high that they vomited before the game. I remember Freddie Biletnikoff was tying his shoes over and over again. He'll do it maybe 50 times before a regular-season game, but that day Freddie must have hit 1,000.

"After the game was over, for the first time I felt real happy for myself. I remember thinking that there are only about six quarterbacks who have ever won the Super Bowl, and now I'm one of them. A great feeling, a great release, an ego balloon. Freddie was crying and Coach Madden was all red and grinning and guys were hugging each other like a bunch of fruits and pouring champagne over each other and then I suddenly had this tremendous urge for a great big plate of scampi and a bottle of Johnnie Red." . . .

THE SNAKE led the Raiders to a win over the Steelers in the 1976 AFC Championship game, and then went on to thump the Vikings in Super Bowl XI.

2004 | THE EYES have it—with the help of great hands—when Marvin Harrison is on the receiving end, as he's been more often than anyone in history but Jerry Rice | *Photograph by* JEFF GROSS

2009 | HIGH-FLYING Cardinal Larry Fitzgerald snagged this 42-yard TD in a wild-card win over Altanta that launched Arizona's Super Bowl run | *Photograph by* JOHN W. MCDONOUGH

WHAT WAS THE LAST TEAM TO PLAY AN ENTIRE SEASON WITHOUT ATTEMPTING A FIELD GOAL? WHAT WAS THE FIRST HELMET LOGO? WHO WERE THE FIRST PLAYERS TO REACH THE HALL OF FAME? IT'S ALL HERE, ALONG WITH HUNDREDS OF OTHER AMAZING FACTS, ASTOUNDING STATS AND DR. Z'S ALL-DECADE TEAMS

The Decades

2008 | RAY LEWIS, a 10-time Pro Bowl selection and perennial force in the middle of the Ravens' defense, represents the latest step in the evolution of the middle linebacker.

>Time Capsule THE 40^s

1948 | STEVE VAN BUREN (15), led the league in rushing yardage and touchdowns in four of his eight seasons with the Eagles.

> DR. Z's ALL DECADE TEAMS

1940s

END	HALFBACK	FULLBACK	QUARTERBACK	HALFBACK	END
DON HUTSON	**STEVE VAN BUREN**	**MARION MOTLEY**	**SID LUCKMAN**	**SPEC SANDERS**	**MAC SPEEDIE**
Mal Kutner	Bill Dudley	Norm Standlee	Otto Graham	Tony Canadeo	Jim Benton
Pete Pihos	George McAfee	Buddy Young	Sammy Baugh	Chet Mutryn	Ken Kavanaugh
TACKLE	GUARD	CENTER	GUARD	TACKLE	KICKER
AL WISTERT	**DANNY FORTMANN**	**BULLDOG TURNER**	**BILL WILLIS**	**BRUISER KINARD**	**HARVEY JOHNSON**
Lou Rymkus	Riley Matheson	Mel Hein	Buster Ramsey	Vic Sears	Ben Agajanian
Al Blozis	Dick Barwegen	Alex Wojciechowicz	Len Younce	Nate Johnson	Bob Waterfield

1920s–30s

END	BLOCKING BACK	TAILBACK	FULLBACK	WINGBACK	END
DON HUTSON	**FATHER LUMPKIN**	**DUTCH CLARK**	**BRONKO NAGURSKI**	**JOHNNY (BLOOD) MCNALLY**	**BILL HEWITT**
Ray Flaherty	Bo Molenda	Benny Friedman	Clarke Hinkle	Ernie Caddel	Lavie Dilweg
Red Badgro	Riley Smith	Cliff Battles	Ernie Nevers	Tony Latone	Dick Plasman
TACKLE	GUARD	CENTER	GUARD	TACKLE	PUNTER-KICKER
CAL HUBBARD	**DANNY FORTMANN**	**MEL HEIN**	**MIKE MICHALSKE**	**TURK EDWARDS**	**PADDY DRISCOLL**
Turk Edwards	George Musso	George Trafton	Walt Kiesling	Duke Slater	Ken Strong
Wilbur (Fats) Henry	Ed Healey	Joe Alexander	Gus Sonnenberg	Link Lyman	Verne Lewellen

> NFL NEWS

THE 1940 CHAMPIONSHIP GAME, in which the Bears defeat the Redskins 73–0, is the first NFL game broadcast nationally on the radio (Red Barber at the mike). The Mutual Broadcasting System paid $2,500 for the rights.

ELMER LAYDEN, Notre Dame's head coach and athletic director, is elected as the NFL's first commissioner, in 1941.

IN 1943 the NFL mandates that every player on the field must wear a helmet.

THE LIONS AND GIANTS play to a 0–0 tie on Nov. 7, 1943 in Detroit, the last scoreless game in NFL history.

BILL DUDLEY of the Steelers wins the 1945 MVP by leading the NFL in rushing, interceptions and punt returns.

THE DEFENDING CHAMPION RAMS move from Cleveland to Los Angeles for the 1946 season.

THE ALL-AMERICA FOOTBALL CONFERENCE begins play in 1946. In a merger four years later, the San Francisco 49ers, Cleveland Browns and Baltimore Colts join the NFL.

IN 1946 Woody Strode and Kenny Washington sign with the Rams to become the first African-Americans to play in the NFL since '33. Marion Motley and Bill Willis break the color barrier in the AAFC that same season, signing with the Browns.

IN 1948 officials other than referees are issued whistles to replace the horns that had been part of their standard equipment.

IN 1948 Rams halfback Fred Gehrke paints horns on his helmet, the first headgear logo in NFL history.

> NICKNAMES <

[Slingin'] Sammy Baugh
Edward [Ty] Coon
Bob [Twenty Grand] Davis
Gil [Cactus Face] Duggan
Nello [Flash] Falaschi
Kenneth [Kayo] Lunday
Earle [Greasy] Neale
Bob [Stoneface] Waterfield
∧ [Squirmin] Herman Wedemeyer
Bill [Bubbles] Young

RECORD OF THE DECADE

The Chicago Bears scored 258 points in 1944, placing second in the league—a pedestrian statistic until you consider that those Bears are still the only team since 1938 to play an entire season without attempting a field goal.

> GO FIGURE

50,000 Fee, in dollars, for a franchise to join the National Football League in 1940.

1,000 Rushing total, in yards, surpassed by Steve Van Buren of the Eagles and Tony Canadeo of the Packers in 1949, the first time two runners gained 1,000 yards in the same season.

7 Touchdown passes thrown by Bears quarterback Sid Luckman in a 1943 game against the New York Giants—a record equaled four times.

638 Number of NFL players, coaches and front office personnel who served in the U.S. military during World War II, including 22 who were killed in action.

0 First downs picked up by the Giants in a 1942 game against the Redskins, which New York won, 14–7, Washington's only loss of the season.

47 Number of catches separating Don Hutson (74) and the second leading receiver, Pop Ivy, during the 1942 season.

51.4 Average, in yards, of Sammy Baugh's punts in 1940, still the NFL record.

5 Weeks in 1941 that Buff Donelli coached both the Duquesne University football team and the Pittsburgh Steelers before he was forced to choose by the NFL. He picked Duquesne.

64 Percentage of players in 1949 who worked in the off-season.

7 Field goals made, in 15 tries, in 1949 by Bears rookie kicker George Blanda, who went on to play a record 26 years in the NFL.

DECADE HIGHS

RUSHING
YARDS: **4,904** / **STEVE VAN BUREN**
TDS: **59** / **STEVE VAN BUREN**

PASSING
YARDS: **17,002** / **SAMMY BAUGH**
TDS: **149** / **SAMMY BAUGH**

RECEIVING
CATCHES: **329** / **DON HUTSON**
YARDS: **5,089** / **DON HUTSON**
TDS: **63** / **DON HUTSON**

SCORING
589 POINTS / **DON HUTSON**

SEASON HIGHS

RUSHING
YARDS: **1,146** / **STEVE VAN BUREN** 1949
TDS: **15** / **STEVE VAN BUREN** 1945

PASSING
YARDS: **2,938** / **SAMMY BAUGH** 1947
TDS: **28** / **SID LUCKMAN** 1943

RECEIVING
CATCHES: **77** / **TOM FEARS** 1949
YARDS: **1,211** / **DON HUTSON** 1942
TDS: **17** / **DON HUTSON** 1942

SCORING
138 POINTS / **DON HUTSON** 1942

GAME HIGHS

RUSHING
205 YARDS / **STEVE VAN BUREN** 11/27/49

PASSING
468 YARDS / **JOHNNY LUJACK** 12/11/49

RECEIVING
303 YARDS / **JIM BENTON** 11/22/45

SCORING
31 POINTS / **DON HUTSON, 4 TDs,**
7 EXTRA POINTS 10/7/45

>Time Capsule THE 50^S

1959 | FRANK GIFFORD earned his ticket to Canton as a multithreat back, piling up more yards receiving than rushing and even throwing for 14 TDs during his Giants career.

> DR. Z's ALL DECADE TEAM

OFFENSE

END	HALFBACK	QUARTERBACK	FULLBACK	HALFBACK	END
ELROY HIRSCH	**HUGH McELHENNY**	**JOHNNY UNITAS**	**JIM BROWN**	**FRANK GIFFORD**	**RAYMOND BERRY**
Harlon Hill	Ollie Matson	Otto Graham	Joe Perry	Dan Towler	Billy Wilson
Billy Howton	Lenny Moore	Norm Van Brocklin	Tank Younger	Doak Walker	Tom Fears

GUARD	TACKLE	CENTER	TACKLE	GUARD	KICKER
DUANE PUTNAM	**MIKE McCORMACK**	**FRANK GATSKI**	**ROOSEVELT BROWN**	**DICK STANFEL**	**LOU GROZA**
Abe Gibron	Jim Parker	Jim Ringo	Lou Creekmur	Dick Barwegen	Fred Cone
Stan Jones	Lou Groza	Bill Johnson	Bob St. Clair	Bruno Banducci	Sam Baker

DEFENSE

HALFBACK	END	TACKLE	TACKLE	END	HALFBACK
DICK (NIGHT TRAIN) LANE	**GINO MARCHETTI**	**ART DONOVAN**	**ERNIE STAUTNER**	**LEN FORD**	**JACK BUTLER**
Tom Landry	Doug Atkins	Gene (Big Daddy) Lipscomb	Leo Nomellini	Andy Robustelli	Jim David
Don Paul	Gene Brito	Arnie Weinmeister	Bob Gain	Norm Willey	Warren Lahr

SAFETY	LINEBACKER	MIDDLE GUARD	LINEBACKER	SAFETY	PUNTER
EMLEN TUNNELL	**JOE SCHMIDT**	**BILL WILLIS**	**BILL GEORGE**	**BOBBY DILLON**	**HORACE GILLOM**
Jack Christiansen	Chuck Bednarik	Dale Dodrill	George Connor	Yale Lary	Pat Brady
Jimmy Patton	Sam Huff	Les Bingaman	Les Richter	Jerry Norton	Sam Baker

> NFL NEWS

THE FREE SUBSTITUTION RULE is permanently adopted at the start of the 1950 season, making possible the evolution of separate offensive and defensive units.

THE LOS ANGELES RAMS televise all of their games in the 1950 season, the first team to do so. Their attendance drops by 46% from the previous year.

BURT LANCASTER plays the title role in *Jim Thorpe—All American*, the story of the great multisport athlete who was also the first league president of the American Professional Football Association, which would become the National Football League.

THE 1951 CHAMPIONSHIP GAME between the Browns and the Rams is the first nationally televised game. The DuMont Network paid $75,000 for the rights to air the 24–17 Rams win.

THE 1–11 DALLAS TEXANS, operated by the league out of Hershey, Pa., but without a stadium during the second half of the 1952 season, disband at the end of the year. No NFL franchise has gone out of business since.

IN 1953 the United States District Court for the Eastern District of Pennsylvania upholds NFL restrictions on broadcasts of home games into the territory of a team during those games. Commissioner Bert Bell rules in '56 that all home games would be blacked out.

ALAN AMECHE scores the overtime touchdown that ends the Baltimore Colts' 1958 NFL Championship Game against the New York Giants and then appears later that night on *Toast of the Town*, a nationally broadcast variety television show hosted by Ed Sullivan.

> NICKNAMES <

Chuck [Concrete Charlie] Bednarik
Howard [Hopalong] Cassady
L.G. [Long Gone] Dupre
Frank [Gunner] Gatski
Lou [the Toe] Groza
∧ Elroy [Crazy Legs] Hirsch
Dick [Night Train] Lane
Eugene [Big Daddy] Lipscomb
Joe [the Jet] Perry
Zollie [Tug Boat] Toth
Tom [the Bomb] Tracy

RECORD OF THE DECADE

Rams rookie defensive back Dick (Night Train) Lane intercepted a record 14 passes during the 12 games of the 1952 season. More than half a century later, with teams now playing 16 games, Lane's record still stands.

> GO FIGURE

5 | NFL players featured on the cover of SPORTS ILLUSTRATED in the 1950s after San Francisco 49ers quarterback Y.A. Tittle became the first, on the Nov. 22, 1954.

6 | Touchdowns by Cleveland halfback Dub Jones in a 42–21 win over the Bears in 1951, including scores on each of his last five touches.

53,676 | Attendance for the first Pro Bowl, in 1951. The American Conference beat the National Conference 28–27.

4 | AAFC teams that did not join the NFL in 1950. The Brooklyn–New York Yankees, Buffalo Bills, Chicago Hornets and Los Angeles Dons were disbanded and their players were dispersed among the NFL's clubs.

8 | Number of clubs in the American Football League, formed in 1959 and scheduled to begin play in 1960. The original AFL cities were Boston, Buffalo, Dallas, Denver, Houston, Los Angeles, Minneapolis and New York.

375 | Combined NFL head coaching victories (including four Super Bowls) for Tom Landry and Vince Lombardi, who in 1954 worked together under coach Jim Lee Howell as the Giants' defensive and offensive coordinators, respectively.

8 | Interceptions thrown by Chicago Cardinals quarterback Jim Hardy in an opening day loss to the Philadelphia Eagles in 1950. At the time Hardy held the NFL record for most consecutive passes without an interception (114).

5,000 | Minimum wage, in dollars, negotiated in 1957 by the newly established Players' Association.

DECADE HIGHS

RUSHING
YARDS: 7,151 / JOE PERRY
TDs: 49 / JOE PERRY

PASSING
YARDS: 20,539 / NORM VAN BROCKLIN
TDs: 151 / BOBBY LAYNE

RECEIVING
CATCHES: 404 / BILLY WILSON
YARDS: 6,091 / BILLY HOWTON
TDs: 49 / ELROY HIRSCH

SCORING
742 POINTS / LOU GROZA

SEASON HIGHS

RUSHING
YARDS: 1,527 / JIM BROWN 1958
TDs: 17 / JIM BROWN 1958

PASSING
YARDS: 2,899 / JOHNNY UNITAS 1959
TDs: 32 / JOHNNY UNITAS 1959

RECEIVING
CATCHES: 84 / TOM FEARS 1950
YARDS: 1,495 / ELROY HIRSCH 1951
TDs: 17 / ELROY HIRSCH 1951

SCORING
128 POINTS / DOAK WALKER 1950

GAME HIGHS

RUSHING
237 YARDS / JIM BROWN 11/24/57

PASSING
554 YARDS / NORM VAN BROCKLIN 9/28/51

RECEIVING
302 YARDS / CLOYCE BOX 12/3/50

SCORING
36 POINTS / DUB JONES, 6 TDs 11/25/51

>Time Capsule THE 60^s

1969 | DEACON JONES (75), an obscure 14th-round draft pick in '61, emerged as a perennial all-pro defensive end for the Rams.

> DR. Z's ALL DECADE TEAM

OFFENSE

WIDE RECEIVER	HALFBACK	QUARTERBACK	FULLBACK	WIDE RECEIVER	KICKER
LANCE ALWORTH	**GALE SAYERS**	**JOHNNY UNITAS**	**JIM BROWN**	**DON MAYNARD**	**JAN STENERUD**
Tommy McDonald	Lenny Moore	Len Dawson	Jim Taylor	Bobby Mitchell	Jim Bakken
Paul Warfield	Clemon Daniels	Joe Namath	Matt Snell	Bob Hayes	Bruce Gossett

GUARD	TACKLE	CENTER	TACKLE	GUARD	TIGHT END
JIM PARKER	**FORREST GREGG**	**JIM OTTO**	**RON MIX**	**BILLY SHAW**	**MIKE DITKA**
Walt Sweeney	Bob Brown	Jim Ringo	Roosevelt Brown	Gene Hickerson	John Mackey
Fuzzy Thurston	Winston Hill	Mick Tingelhoff	Jim Tyrer	Ed Budde	Pete Retzlaff

DEFENSE

CORNERBACK	END	TACKLE	TACKLE	END	CORNERBACK
JIMMY JOHNSON	**DEACON JONES**	**MERLIN OLSEN**	**BOB LILLY**	**RICH JACKSON**	**WILLIE BROWN**
Dick (Night Train) Lane	Gino Marchetti	Alex Karras	Houston Antwine	Willie Davis	Herb Adderley
Dick LeBeau	Doug Atkins	Tom Sestak	Henry Jordan	Earl Faison	Lem Barney

STRONG SAFETY	LINEBACKER	LINEBACKER	LINEBACKER	FREE SAFETY	PUNTER
RICHIE PETITBON	**DAVE WILCOX**	**DICK BUTKUS**	**CHUCK HOWLEY**	**LARRY WILSON**	**TOMMY DAVIS**
Johnny Robinson	Dave Robinson	Ray Nitschke	Bobby Bell	Willie Wood	Yale Lary
Kenny Graham	Wayne Walker	Lee Roy Jordan	Larry Grantham	Eddie Meador	Jerrel Wilson

> NFL NEWS

BYRON (WHIZZER) WHITE, the NFL's rushing leader in 1940, is appointed to the United States Supreme Court in '62.

THE PRO FOOTBALL Hall of Fame opens in Canton, Ohio, in 1963.

PETE GOGOLAK of Cornell becomes the first professional soccer-style kicker when he signs with the Bills in 1964.

ON OCT. 25, 1964, defensive end Jim Marshall picks up a 49ers fumble and rambles 66 yards into the end zone for what he thinks is a touchdown. Marshall ran the wrong way, however, and scored two points for San Francisco.

OAKLAND'S COACH AND G.M. Al Davis becomes commissioner of the AFL in 1966.

IN THE SPRING OF 1966 Tex Schramm of the Cowboys and Lamar Hunt of the Chiefs hold secret meetings to work out the details of a merger between the AFL and NFL for the 1970 season.

WHILE FILMING *The Dirty Dozen*, Jim Brown, 30, the NFL's alltime leading rusher, announces that he's retiring from football to pursue acting full time.

FORMER GIANTS DEFENSIVE BACK Emlen Tunnell becomes the first African-American elected to the Pro Football Hall of Fame.

ON NOV. 17, 1968, NBC switches from its national broadcast of the Jets-Raiders game with 50 seconds remaining to air the children's movie *Heidi*. The Jets are leading 32–29 at the time, but Oakland scores two TDs to win 43–32 while calls from legions of irate viewers overwhelm the NBC switchboard in Manhattan.

> NICKNAMES <

Lance [Bambi] Alworth
Junious [Buck] Buchanan
Elbert [Golden Wheels] Dubenion
Carlton [Cookie] Gilchrist
David [Deacon] Jones
Daryle [the Mad Bomber] Lamonica
Jim [Wrong Way] Marshall
[Broadway] Joe Namath
∧ Charles [Bubba] Smith
Fred [Fuzzy] Thurston
Fred [Hammer] Williamson

RECORD OF THE DECADE

Bears rookie Gale Sayers set an NFL record for touchdowns in a season by getting into the end zone 22 times in 1965. Sayers reached pay dirt 14 times on the ground, six times through the air and twice on returns (one punt, one kickoff).

> GO FIGURE

17 | Points by which the NFL's Baltimore Colts were favored over the AFL's New York Jets in Super Bowl III. The Jets won, 16–7.

23 | Number of ballots it took NFL owners to elect Pete Rozelle commissioner in 1960.

15,000 | Winning player's share, in dollars, for the Green Bay Packers from the AFL–NFL World Championship Game (a.k.a. Super Bowl I), played in Los Angeles on Jan. 15, 1967.

14 | Regular-season NFL games after two were added to each team's 1961 schedule.

2,000 | Dollars paid in fines by Detroit's Alex Karras and Green Bay's Paul Hornung in 1963 for placing bets on NFL games. They were also were suspended indefinitely and sat out one year.

2 | Days after the assassination of President Kennedy that the NFL allowed games to be played. Three of the seven games played that day were sellouts.

22 | Consecutive games, from 1963 to '65, in which Colts back Lenny Moore scored a touchdown.

18 | Consecutive games during the 1962 and '63 seasons in which Raiders defensive back Tom Morrow had an interception.

17 | Charter members of the Pro Football Hall of Fame when it opened in 1963: Sammy Baugh, Bert Bell, Joe Carr, Earl (Dutch) Clark, Red Grange, George Halas, Mel Hein, Wilbur (Fats) Henry, Cal Hubbard, Don Hutson, Earl (Curly) Lambeau, Tim Mara, George Preston Marshall, Johnny (Blood) McNally, Bronko Nagurski, Ernie Nevers and Jim Thorpe.

DECADE HIGHS

RUSHING
YARDS: **8,514** / **JIM BROWN**
TDS: **76** / **JIM TAYLOR**

PASSING
YARDS: **26,548** / **JOHNNY UNITAS**
TDS: **207** / **SONNY JURGENSEN**

RECEIVING
CATCHES: **470** / **BOBBY MITCHELL**
YARDS: **7,472** / **BOBBY MITCHELL**
TDS: **64** / **SONNY RANDLE**

SCORING
870 POINTS / **LOU MICHAELS**

SEASON HIGHS

RUSHING
YARDS: **1,863** / **JIM BROWN** 1963
TDS: **19** / **JIM TAYLOR** 1962

PASSING
YARDS: **3,747** / **SONNY JURGENSEN** 1967
TDS: **36** / **Y.A. TITTLE** 1963

RECEIVING
CATCHES: **93** / **JOHNNY MORRIS** 1964
YARDS: **1,436** / **BOBBY MITCHELL** 1963
TDS: **15** / **SONNY RANDLE** 1960

SCORING
176 POINTS / **PAUL HORNUNG** 1960

GAME HIGHS

RUSHING
237 YARDS / **JIM BROWN** 11/19/61

PASSING
505 YARDS / **Y.A. TITTLE** 10/28/62

RECEIVING
269 YARDS / **DEL SHOFNER** 10/28/62

SCORING
36 POINTS / **GALE SAYERS, 6 TDs** 12/12/65

> Time Capsule THE 70ˢ

1972 | FRANCO HARRIS was a seven-time All-Pro running back and the MVP of Super Bowl IX, one of the Steelers' four title-game wins in the decade.

HEINZ KLUETMEIER (2)

> DR. Z's ALL DECADE TEAM

OFFENSE

WIDE RECEIVER	RUNNING BACK	QUARTERBACK	FULLBACK	WIDE RECEIVER	KICKER
HAROLD CARMICHAEL	**WALTER PAYTON**	**ROGER STAUBACH**	**LARRY CSONKA**	**HAROLD JACKSON**	**GARO YEPREMIAN**
Cliff Branch	O.J. Simpson	Ken Anderson	Sam Cunningham	Fred Biletnikoff	Don Cockroft
Charlie Joiner	Franco Harris	Terry Bradshaw	Rocky Bleier	Lynn Swann	Mark Moseley
GUARD	TACKLE	CENTER	TACKLE	GUARD	TIGHT END
JOHN HANNAH	**ART SHELL**	**MIKE WEBSTER**	**RAYFIELD WRIGHT**	**BOB KUECHENBERG**	**DAVE CASPER**
Gene Upshaw	Jon Kolb	Jim Langer	Winston Hill	Bob Young	Charlie Sanders
Doug Wilkerson	Dan Dierdorf	Dave Dalby	George Kunz	Tom Mack	Ray Chester

DEFENSE

CORNERBACK	END	TACKLE	TACKLE	END	CORNERBACK
JAMES JOHNSON	**CEDRICK HARDMAN**	**JOE GREENE**	**BOB LILLY**	**ELVIN BETHEA**	**WILLIE BROWN**
Mike Haynes	L.C. Greenwood	Curley Culp	Alan Page	Jack Youngblood	Mel Blount
Mel Renfro	Claude Humphrey	Randy White	Ernie Holmes	Carl Eller	Roger Wehrli
STRONG SAFETY	LINEBACKER	LINEBACKER	LINEBACKER	FREE SAFETY	PUNTER
KEN HOUSTON	**TED HENDRICKS**	**WILLIE LANIER**	**JACK HAM**	**CLIFF HARRIS**	**RAY GUY**
Charlie Waters	Matt Blair	Jack Lambert	Dave Wilcox	Jake Scott	Jerrel Wilson
Dick Anderson	Robert Brazile	Lee Roy Jordan	Tom Jackson	Paul Krause	Dave Jennings

> NFL NEWS

ABC'S *MONDAY NIGHT FOOTBALL* makes its debut on Sept. 21, 1970, with a game between the Browns and the Jets.

PRESIDENT RICHARD NIXON makes national news by suggesting plays for the 1971 postseason to Redskins coach George Allen and Dolphins coach Don Shula.

ON JULY 13, 1972, Carroll Rosenbloom, who owned the Colts, and Robert Irsay, who had recently taken over the Los Angeles Rams, swap franchises.

CONGRESS ADOPTS LEGISLATION requiring that any NFL game sold out 72 hours before kickoff must be made available on local TV.

PASSER RATING becomes an official NFL statistic in 1973.

THE WORLD FOOTBALL LEAGUE begins play in 1974. A year later Miami's "Butch Cassidy and The Sundance Kid" backfield of Larry Csonka and Jim Kiick, along with receiver Paul Warfield, sign with the Memphis Southmen after contract disputes with the Dolphins.

DOLPHINS QUARTERBACK BOB GRIESE, in 1977, becomes the first NFL player to wear glasses during a game.

RAIDERS TIGHT END Dave Casper bats a loose ball into the end zone and pounces on it to score a game-winning touchdown against the Chargers in 1978. The play, dubbed the Holy Roller, is outlawed the following season.

OILERS ROOKIE Earl Campbell gains 1,450 yards on the ground in 1978 and becomes the first rookie since Jim Brown ('57) to top the NFL in rushing yards.

> NICKNAMES <

Sam [Bam] Cunningham
John [Frenchy] Fuqua
[Mean Joe] Greene
Thomas [Hollywood] Henderson
Ted [the Mad Stork] Hendricks
∧ Billy [White Shoes] Johnson
Ed [Too Tall] Jones
Carl [Spider] Lockhart
Eugene [Mercury] Morris
Jack [Hacksaw] Reynolds
Ken [Snake] Stabler

RECORD OF THE DECADE

Vikings defensive end Jim Marshall established an alltime record by playing in 282 consecutive games. Marshall's streak began in 1960, during the Eisenhower Administration, and ended in 1979, with Jimmy Carter in office.

> GO FIGURE

6 | Professional heavyweight fights for Cowboys defensive end Ed (Too Tall) Jones during his one-year hiatus from football in 1979. He won all his bouts, five by KO.

63 | Length, in yards, of field goal by New Orleans kicker Tom Dempsey against the Lions on Nov. 8, 1970, the longest in NFL history.

26 | Consecutive losses by Tampa Bay Buccaneers, a streak that began with the team's inaugural game in 1976.

5 | Consecutive losses by the Seattle Seahawks in 1976, a streak that began with the team's inaugural game. Seattle's first win came against Tampa Bay.

2,003 | Yards gained in 1973 in 14 games by Bills running back O.J. Simpson, the first man to rush for more than 2,000 yards in a season.

17 | Consecutive wins for the 1972 Miami Dolphins, the only team to win every game through the regular season, the playoffs and the Super Bowl.

82:40 | Official game time needed to complete Christmas Day playoff in 1971 between the Dolphins and the Chiefs. Garo Yepremian's field goal gave Miami the win in the longest game in NFL history.

98 | Yards gained on the longest nonscoring play in NFL history when Cardinals wide receiver Bobby Moore (later known as Ahmad Rashad) caught a Jim Hart pass in a 1972 game against the Rams but was pulled down one yard short of the end zone.

DECADE HIGHS

RUSHING
YARDS: **10,539** / O.J. SIMPSON
TDs: **72** / FRANCO HARRIS

PASSING
YARDS: **23,863** / FRAN TARKENTON
TDs: **156** / FRAN TARKENTON

RECEIVING
CATCHES: **432** / HAROLD JACKSON
YARDS: **7,724** / HAROLD JACKSON
TDs: **61** / HAROLD JACKSON

SCORING
905 POINTS / GARO YEPREMIAN

SEASON HIGHS

RUSHING
YARDS: **2,003** / O.J. SIMPSON 1973
TDs: **19** / EARL CAMPBELL 1979

PASSING
YARDS: **4,082** / DAN FOUTS 1979
TDs: **28** / TERRY BRADSHAW 1978,
STEVE GROGAN and BRIAN SIPE 1979

RECEIVING
CATCHES: **88** / RICKEY YOUNG 1978
YARDS: **1,237** / STEVE LARGENT 1979
TDs: **13** / DICK GORDON 1970, HAROLD JACKSON 1973,
CLIFF BRANCH 1974, JOHN JEFFERSON 1978

SCORING
138 POINTS / O.J. SIMPSON 1975

GAME HIGHS

RUSHING
275 YARDS / WALTER PAYTON 11/20/77

PASSING
496 YARDS / JOE NAMATH 9/24/72

RECEIVING
255 YARDS / JERRY BUTLER 9/23/79

SCORING
24 POINTS / WILBERT MONTGOMERY, 4 TDs
9/10/78 and 10/7/79; **19 OTHERS** (once each)

>Time Capsule THE 90ˢ

1998 | REGGIE WHITE (92), the Minister of Defense, was one of the league's most fearsome pass rushers for more than a decade.

> DR. Z's ALL DECADE TEAM

OFFENSE

WIDE RECEIVER	RUNNING BACK	QUARTERBACK	FULLBACK	WIDE RECEIVER	KICKER
JERRY RICE	**EMMITT SMITH**	**STEVE YOUNG**	**DARYL JOHNSTON**	**CRIS CARTER**	**MORTEN ANDERSEN**
Andre Reed	Barry Sanders	John Elway	Mike Alstott	Sterling Sharpe	Nick Lowery
Irving Fryar	Thurman Thomas	Troy Aikman	Larry Centers	Michael Irvin	John Carney
GUARD	TACKLE	CENTER	TACKLE	GUARD	TIGHT END
LARRY ALLEN	**MIKE KENN**	**DERMONTTI DAWSON**	**JACKIE SLATER**	**BRUCE MATTHEWS**	**SHANNON SHARPE**
Dave Szott	Tony Boselli	Kent Hull	Bruce Armstrong	Will Shields	Ben Coates
Randall McDaniel	Harris Barton	Tom Nalen	Gary Zimmerman	Steve Wisniewski	Jay Novacek

DEFENSE

CORNERBACK	END	TACKLE	TACKLE	END	CORNERBACK
DEION SANDERS	**REGGIE WHITE**	**BRYANT YOUNG**	**CORTEZ KENNEDY**	**BRUCE SMITH**	**DARRELL GREEN**
Rod Woodson	Charles Haley	Ray Childress	Warren Sapp	Robert Porcher	Albert Lewis
Aeneas Williams	Leslie O'Neal	Michael Dean Perry	Dan Saleaumua	Neil Smith	Dwayne Harper
STRONG SAFETY	LINEBACKER	LINEBACKER	LINEBACKER	FREE SAFETY	PUNTER
TIM McDONALD	**DERRICK BROOKS**	**RAY LEWIS**	**DERRICK THOMAS**	**BRIAN DAWKINS**	**MATT TURK**
LeRoy Butler	Junior Seau	Sam Mills	Seth Joyner	Eugene Robinson	Darren Bennett
Rodney Harrison	Kevin Greene	Chris Spielman	Rickey Jackson	Merton Hanks	Rich Camarillo

> NFL NEWS

FOX OUTBIDS CBS for the NFC broadcast package and begins televising games in 1994. Four years later CBS takes the AFC from NBC with a staggering $17.6 billion, eight-year deal.

DON SHULA wins his 325th game, on Nov. 14, 1993, to surpass George Halas as the winningest NFL coach. The Dolphins coach would retire after the 1995 season with 347 wins.

IN 1994, a year before his induction into the Hall of Fame, former Seattle Seahawks wideout Steve Largent is elected to the U.S. Congress to represent the first district of Oklahoma.

THE NFL becomes the first major pro league with its own dedicated website when it launches NFLhome.com on April 10, 1995.

ON OCT. 3, 1995 Pro Football Hall of Famer O.J. Simpson is found not guilty of murdering his ex-wife, Nicole Brown Simpson, and her friend Ronald Goldman. Simpson is later found liable for the wrongful deaths in a civil suit filed by the victims' families and is ordered to pay $33.5 million.

FOUR TEAMS RELOCATE: the Rams (Anaheim to St. Louis), the Raiders (Los Angeles to Oakland), the Oilers (Houston to Nashville by way of Memphis) and the Browns/Ravens (Cleveland to Baltimore).

ON OCT. 25, 1998, Jason Elam of the Denver Broncos kicks a 63-yard field goal, tying the record set by Tom Dempsey of the New Orleans Saints in 1970.

THE NFL'S 29TH AND 30TH FRANCHISES, the Carolina Panthers and the Jacksonville Jaguars, begin play in 1995 and reach conference championship games in their second seasons. The expansion Browns begin play in 1999.

> NICKNAMES <

Jerome [the Bus] Bettis
Craig [Ironhead] Heyward
Qadry [the Missile] Ismail
Ragib [the Rocket] Ismail
Thomas [Pepper] Johnson
Nate [the Kitchen] Newton
∧ Andre [Bad Moon] Rison
Deion [Prime Time] Sanders
Rick [Bootin'] Tuten
Reggie [the Minister of Defense] White

RECORD OF THE DECADE

No team had ever won its conference championship four years in a row or appeared in four straight Super Bowls—let alone *lost* all four—before the Buffalo Bills of 1990–93 were beaten by the Giants, the Redskins and the Cowboys (twice) in consecutive title games.

> GO FIGURE

1,457 Yards Barry Sanders needed to tie Walter Payton as the NFL's all-time leading rusher when the Lions running back abruptly retired before the 1999 season, at the age of 31.

22 Penalties (for a total of 178 yards) committed by the 49ers in their 26–21 loss to the Bills in 1998. That tied the single-game record set by the Brooklyn Dodgers and tied later by the Chicago Bears, both in 1944.

195 Players drafted in 1995 ahead of Terrell Davis, who becomes the lowest draft choice to rush for 1,000 yards in his first season with the Denver Broncos.

7 Rounds to which the NFL draft was reduced in 1994, down from eight the previous year and 12 from 1977 to 1992.

6 Consecutive 300-yard passing games by San Francisco 49ers quarterback Steve Young in 1999, breaking the NFL record of five by former teammate Joe Montana.

12 Rank at which *The Dark Side of the Game*, a 1996 novel by former Atlanta Falcons linebacker Tim Green, made its debut on *The New York Times* best sellers list.

51 Years between playoff wins for the Cardinals franchise after Arizona defeats the Dallas Cowboys, 20–7, in a 1998 NFC wild-card game.

15 Wins during the 1998 regular season by the Vikings, who joined the '84 49ers and '85 Bears as the only teams to win that many in a single year. Minnesota alone, however, failed to win the Super Bowl, losing the NFC title game in overtime to the Falcons.

DECADE HIGHS

RUSHING
YARDS: 13,963 / EMMITT SMITH
TDS: 136 / EMMITT SMITH

PASSING
YARDS: 33,508 / DAN MARINO
TDS: 235 / BRETT FAVRE

RECEIVING
CATCHES: 860 / JERRY RICE
YARDS: 12,078 / JERRY RICE
TDS: 103 / JERRY RICE

SCORING
1,130 POINTS / GARY ANDERSON

SEASON HIGHS

RUSHING
YARDS: 2,053 / BARRY SANDERS 1997
TDS: 25 / EMMITT SMITH 1995

PASSING
YARDS: 4,690 / WARREN MOON 1991
TDS: 41 / KURT WARNER 1999

RECEIVING
CATCHES: 123 / HERMAN MOORE 1995
YARDS: 1,848 / JERRY RICE 1995
TDS: 18 / STERLING SHARPE 1994

SCORING
164 POINTS / GARY ANDERSON 1998

GAME HIGHS

RUSHING
246 YARDS / COREY DILLON 12/4/97

PASSING
527 YARDS / WARREN MOON 12/16/90

RECEIVING
289 YARDS / JERRY RICE 12/18/95

SCORING
30 POINTS / JERRY RICE, 5 TDs 10/14/90
JAMES STEWART, 5 TDs 10/12/97

>Time Capsule THE 00ˢ

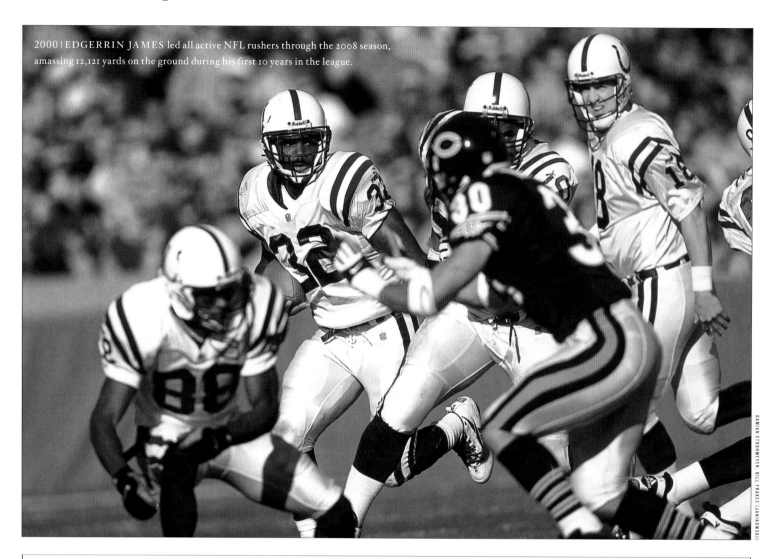

2000 | EDGERRIN JAMES led all active NFL rushers through the 2008 season, amassing 12,121 yards on the ground during his first 10 years in the league.

DAMIAN STROHMEYER, BILL FRAKES (JANKOWSKI)

> DR. Z's ALL DECADE TEAM

OFFENSE

WIDE RECEIVER	RUNNING BACK	QUARTERBACK	FULLBACK	WIDE RECEIVER	KICKER
MARVIN HARRISON	**LADAINIAN TOMLINSON**	**TOM BRADY**	**TONY RICHARDSON**	**RANDY MOSS**	**ADAM VINATIERI**
Hines Ward	Shaun Alexander	Peyton Manning	Lorenzo Neal	Torry Holt	David Akers
Larry Fitzgerald	Marshall Faulk	Brett Favre	Mike Alstott	Steve Smith	Stephen Gostkowski

GUARD	TACKLE	CENTER	TACKLE	GUARD	TIGHT END
ALAN FANECA	**WALTER JONES**	**KEVIN MAWAE**	**WILLIE ROAF**	**STEVE HUTCHINSON**	**TONY GONZALEZ**
Logan Mankins	Jonathan Ogden	Olin Kreutz	Orlando Pace	Mike Wahle	Antonio Gates
Marco Rivera	Brad Hopkins	Jeff Saturday	Willie Anderson	Will Shields	Jason Witten

DEFENSE

CORNERBACK	END	TACKLE	TACKLE	END	CORNERBACK
TY LAW	**MICHAEL STRAHAN**	**LA'ROI GLOVER**	**RICHARD SEYMOUR**	**JASON TAYLOR**	**CHAMP BAILEY**
Asante Samuel	Patrick Kerney	Jamal Williams	Albert Haynesworth	Jared Allen	Troy Vincent
Ronde Barber	Dwight Freeney	Kevin Williams	Seth Payne	Aaron Kampman	Nate Clements

STRONG SAFETY	LINEBACKER	LINEBACKER	LINEBACKER	FREE SAFETY	PUNTER
BOB SANDERS	**DERRICK BROOKS**	**RAY LEWIS**	**DeMARCUS WARE**	**ED REED**	**MIKE SCIFRES**
Darren Woodson	Keith Bulluck	Zach Thomas	Brian Urlacher	Brian Dawkins	Brian Moorman
John Lynch	Joey Porter	Tedy Bruschi	Shawne Merriman	Darren Sharper	Shane Lechler

> NFL NEWS

NFL EXECUTIVE VICE PRESIDENT and chief operating officer Roger Goodell is named NFL commissioner on Aug. 8, 2006. Goodell, who began his NFL career as an intern in 1982, succeeds Paul Tagliabue, who had served in the position since '89.

VIKINGS OFFENSIVE tackle Korey Stringer collapses from heatstroke during training camp, on July 31, 2001, and dies the next day.

IN THE FIRST NFL playoff game to take place in February, Super Bowl XXXVI is decided on the final play. Adam Vinatieri's 48-yard field goal gives the Patriots a 20–17 win over the Rams.

THE EXPANSION Houston Texans join the NFL in 2002. The Seattle Seahawks move from the AFC to the NFC as the league realigns into eight four-team divisions.

RETURN SPECIALIST Chad Morton takes the overtime kickoff 96 yards for a touchdown, as the Jets defeat the Bills on Sept. 8, 2002 in the shortest OT (14 seconds) since the extra period was introduced in regular season games in 1974.

THE COWBOYS' Emmitt Smith becomes the NFL's alltime leading rusher, surpassing Walter Payton's career mark on Oct. 27, 2002.

AFTER 35 SEASONS on ABC, the league announces on April 18, 2005, that *Monday Night Football* will move to ESPN in 2006.

FALCONS QB Michael Vick pleads guilty to criminal conspiracy charges relating to his ownership of a dogfighting ring in Surry County, Va. Vick is sentenced on Dec. 10, 2007 to 23 months in federal prison and suspended indefinitely by the league after animal activists protest at NFL headquarters.

> NICKNAMES <

Mike [A-Train] Alstott
⌃ Sebastian [Sea Bass] Janikowski
Adam [Pacman] Jones
Anthony [Booger] McFarland
Shawne [Lights Out] Merriman
Julius [the Matrix] Peppers
Rod [He Hate Me] Smart
Darren [Tank] Sproles
Reggie [Batman] Wayne
Carnell [Cadillac] Williams

RECORD OF THE DECADE

Ravens All-Pro free safety Ed Reed set the NFL record for longest interception return, with a 107-yard runback for a score against the Eagles on Nov. 23, 2008. Reed also held the previous record, set four years earlier with a 106-yard scamper against the Browns.

> GO FIGURE

0 | Losses during the 2007 regular season by the New England Patriots, the first undefeated team since the NFL expanded to a 16-game regular season schedule.

16 | Losses by the 2008 Detroit Lions, the first team to go winless in a 16-game season.

109 | Length, in yards, of an NFL-record return for a TD by Chargers CB Antonio Cromartie after a missed 57-yard field goal during a 2007 game against the Vikings.

74 | NFL record for PATs, set by Patriots kicker Stephen Gostkowski during the 2007 season.

416 | Carries by Chiefs running back Larry Johnson in 2006, breaking the old mark of 410 set by Atlanta's Jamal Anderson in 1998.

3 | Stadiums in which the Saints played 2005 "home" games after Hurricane Katrina struck New Orleans: Giants Stadium (one game), the Alamodome (3) and LSU's Tiger Stadium (4).

165 | Points allowed by the 2000 Super Bowl champion Ravens, the fewest ever by an NFL team in a 16-game season.

22½ | Sacks in 2001 by New York Giants defensive end Michael Strahan, breaking Mark Gastineau's NFL record of 22.

0 | NFL games played on Sept. 16–17, Week 2 of the 2001 season, in the wake of the 9/11 terrorist attacks.

76 | Number of times Texans quarterback David Carr was sacked in 2002, an NFL record.

DECADE HIGHS	SEASON HIGHS	GAME HIGHS
RUSHING	**RUSHING**	**RUSHING**
YARDS: 11,760 / LADAINIAN TOMLINSON	YARDS: 2,066 / JAMAL LEWIS 2003	296 YARDS / ADRIAN PETERSON 11/4/07
TDS: 126 / LADAINIAN TOMLINSON	TDS: 28 / LADAINIAN TOMLINSON 2006	
PASSING	**PASSING**	**PASSING**
YARDS: 37,754 / PEYTON MANNING	YARDS: 5,069 / DREW BREES 2008	510 YARDS / DREW BREES 11/19/06
TDS: 281 / PEYTON MANNING	TDS: 50 / TOM BRADY 2007	
RECEIVING	**RECEIVING**	**RECEIVING**
CATCHES: 817 / TORRY HOLT	CATCHES: 143 / MARVIN HARRISON 2002	291 YARDS / JIMMY SMITH 9/10/00
YARDS: 11,872 / TORRY HOLT	YARDS: 1,722 / MARVIN HARRISON 2002	
TDS: 109 / TERRELL OWENS	TDS: 23 / RANDY MOSS 2007	
SCORING	**SCORING**	**SCORING**
1,069 POINTS / JASON ELAM	186 POINTS / LADAINIAN TOMLINSON 2006	30 POINTS / SHAUN ALEXANDER, 5 TDS 9/29/02
		CLINTON PORTIS, 5 TDS 12/7/03

RECORDS THROUGH THE 2008 SEASON

2008 | LAMBEAU TABLEAU: The Seahawks (right) were pelted with a blizzard of six Packer touchdowns during Green Bay's 42–20 divisional playoff win | *Photograph by* SIMON BRUTY

Acknowledgments

THE WORDS AND PICTURES collected here represent the work of several generations of SPORTS ILLUSTRATED writers, photographers and editors, but this book would not have been possible without the contributions of many current and former members of the SI staff: Stefanie Kaufman, Linda Verigan, Ed Truscio, Chris Hercik, Linda Root, Michele Brea, Steve Fine, Geoff Michaud, Dan Larkin, Bob Thompson, Mary Morel, Annmarie Modugno-Avila, Joy Birdsong, Natasha Simon, Linda Levine, George Amores, Larry Gallop, Ann McCarthy, Karen Carpenter, Gabe Miller, Brian Clavell, Chelsea Cartabiano and Barbara Fox. Invaluable assistance was provided by the Pro Football Hall of Fame, especially by Saleem Choudhry, Jason Aikens and Reuben Canales of NFL/Wireimage. And special thanks to Terry McDonell, Editor of the Sports Illustrated Group, for his unstinting support.

Grateful acknowledgment is also made to the following for permission to reprint copyrighted material:

How Does It Really Feel? Copyright © 1974 by Roy Blount Jr.

The Game That Was and *A Life for Two Tough Texans* Copyright © 1969; *The Immaculate Reception and Other Miracles* Copyright © 1973 by Myron Cope. Used by permission of the estate of Myron Cope.

Zero of the Lions Copyright © 1974. Used by permission of the estate of George Plimpton

The Day of the Game Copyright © 1963 by Vince Lombardi and W.C. Heinz. Reprinted by permission of William Morris Agency LLC on behalf of the author. Copyright © 1963 TM/© 2005 Vince Lombardi by cmgworldwide.com, vincelombardi.com

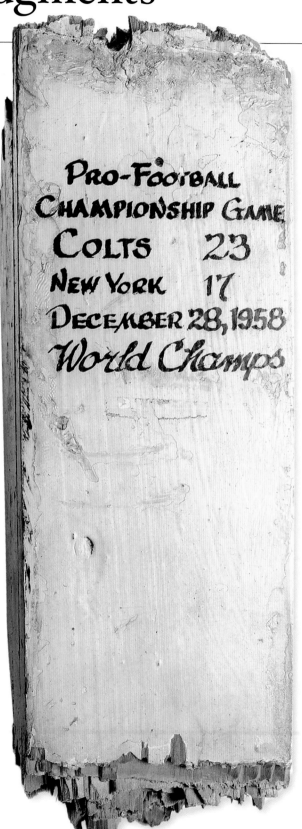

COURTESY OF THE PRO FOOTBALL HALL OF FAME

PRO-FOOTBALL CHAMPIONSHIP GAME
COLTS 23
NEW YORK 17
DECEMBER 28, 1958
World Champs

Photo Credits

Hall of Fame photography by David N. Berkwitz: p. 1, 6, 12, 14, 16, 28, 44, 52, 70, 71, 86, 100, 101, 112, 113, 130, 131, 152, 172, 173, 182, 183, 192, 213, 217, 230, 248, 286, 320. Artifacts courtesy of the Pro Football Hall of Fame.

COVER CREDITS: AP/Wide World Photos 1, John Biever 5, Todd Bigelow/Aurora 1, George Bridges/ KRT/ABACA 1, Peter Brouilett/NFL/Wireimage 1, Simon Bruty 1, Jerome Davis/Icon SMI 1, Albert Dickson/TSN/Icon SMI 1, Tom DiPace 4, Mike Ehrmann/Wireimage 1, James Flores/Wireimage 1, Greg Foster 1, Bill Frakes 2, Rich Frishman 1, George Gojkovich/Getty Images 1, John D. Hanlon 1, Andy Hayt 1, HOF/NFL/Wireimage 1, Kent Horner/AP/ Wide World Photos 1, John Iacono 1, Icon SMI 2, Walter Iooss Jr. 3, Lawrence Jackson/AP/Wide World Photos 1, Glenn James/Wireimage 1, Steve Jacobson 1, Allen Kee/Wireimage 1, Heinz Kluetmeier 2, David E. Klutho 1, Kirby Lee/Wireimage 1, Neil Leifer 8, Fred Lyon 1, Brad Mangin 1, Al Messerschmidt/ Wireimage 3, Manny Millan 2, Peter Read Miller 1, Anthony Neste 1, NFL/Wireimage 1, Michael O'Neill 1, Ken Regan/Camera 5 2, Robert Rogers 1, Bob Rosato 2, Ron Schwane/Icon SMI 1, Marc Serota/Reuters 1, Sportschrome 1, Rich Sugg/Kansas City Star/AP/ Wide World Photos 1, Kevin Terrell/Wireimage 1, Al Tielemans 1, Tony Tomsic 5, Tony Tomsic/US Presswire 2, Joe Traver/Reuters 1, Rob Tringali/Sportschrome 1, Steve Wewerka 1, Frank White 1, John G. Zimmerman 3

TABLE OF CONTENTS *(top to bottom, from left)*: John G. Zimmerman, Neil Leifer, Neil Leifer, Damian Strohmeyer; Al Tielemans, Hy Peskin, Jerry Wachter; Neil Leifer, Walter Iooss Jr., Al Tielemans; John W. McDonough, Tony Tomsic, Andy Hayt, Richard Mackson

PHOTO CREDITS: 1Deuce3 Photography: 102; AP/ Wide World Photos: p. 29, 56, 58, 67, 82, 83, 116, 117, 144, 150, 151, 159, 212, 224 (2), 231, 246, 268, 272, 273, 274, 287, 297; Camera 5: p. 58; Contact Press Images: p. 54, 55; Corbis: p. 90, 91, 193, 232, 233, 291; GT Images: p. 50, 51, 191, 260; Getty Images: p. 20, 30, 31, 69, 74, 118, 206, 242, 243, 288, 294, 295, 301; Icon SMI: p. 59, 127, 247; Milwaukee Journal Sentinel/ AP/Wide World Photos: p. 207; NFL/Wireimage: p. 118, 144, 145, 206, 207, 224; Reuters: p. 186; Sportschrome: p. 119; Time & Life Picture/Getty Images: 2, 8, 9, 10, 11, 146; Topeka Capital-Journal/AP/Wide World Photos: p. 186; TSN/Zuma Press/Icon SMI: 145, 206 (2); TSN/Zuma Press/US Presswire: p. 83, 206; US Presswire: 119, 225 (2), 261; Wireimage: 59, 82, 88, 118 (2), 142, 144, 145, 186, 187, 207, 224

TIME INC. HOME ENTERTAINMENT: Richard Fraiman, PUBLISHER; Steven Sandonato, GENERAL MANAGER; Carol Pittard, EXECUTIVE DIRECTOR, MARKETING SERVICES; Tom Mifsud, DIRECTOR, RETAIL & SPECIAL SALES; Peter Harper, DIRECTOR, NEW PRODUCT DEVELOPMENT; Sydney Webber, DIRECTOR OF TRADE MARKETING; Laura Adam, ASSISTANT DIRECTOR, BOOKAZINE MARKETING; Joy Butts, ASSISTANT DIRECTOR, BRAND MARKETING; Helen Wan, ASSOCIATE COUNSEL; Alexandra Bliss, BRAND & LICENSING MANAGER; Anne-Michelle Gallero, DESIGN & PREPRESS MANAGER; Susan Chodakiewicz, BOOK PRODUCTION MANAGER; Allison Parker, ASSOCIATE BRAND MANAGER

A piece of the goalpost from the NFL's first sudden-death championship game resides in the Hall of Fame, in Canton.

Sports Illustrated